Trea

Treading on Python: Volume 1

Foundations

Matt Harrison

Technical Editor: Shannon -jj Behrens

Contents

Introduction

ARE YOU READY TO JUMPSTART YOUR PYTHON programming career? This book will arm you with years of knowledge and experience are condensed into a easy to follow format. Rather than taking months reading blogs and websites and searching mailing lists and groups, this book will allow a programmer to quickly feel knowledgable and comfortable with Python.

Programming is fun and Python makes it delightful. Basic Python is not only easy, but approachable for all ages. I have taught elementary students, teenagers, "industry" professionals and "golden years" folks the Python programming language. If you are willing to read and type, you are about to begin an exciting path. Where it ultimately takes you depends on how hard you are willing to work.

There are a different levels of Python. Basic Python syntax is small and easy to learn. Once you master basic Python, doors will open to you. You should be able to read a lot of Python and understand it. From there, you can learn more advanced topics and specific toolkits, start contributing to open source projects written in Python, or use that knowledge to learn other programming languages.

A recommended approach for learning the language is to read a chapter then actually sit down at a computer and type out some of the examples found in the chapter. Python makes it easy to get started, eliminating much of the rain dancing found in running programs in other languages. The temptation will likely be to merely read the book. By jumping in and actually typing the examples you will learn a lot more than just reading.

Chapter 1

Why Python?

There are many programming languages, and the popularity of them ebb and flow. In recent years, Python has become quite popular. Those involved with startups, scientific computing, and even large corporations have felt a pull towards Python. Python is a great language to start out with. It is also easy to learn if you know another language.

Python enables productivity. I came to Python as a Perl programmer. At work I was tasked to work with a co-worker who was well versed in Tcl. Neither wanted to jump ship though both of us were interested in learning Python. In 3 days our prototype was completed, much faster than we expected, and we both promptly forgot our previous "goto" language. What appealed to me about Python was that it fit my brain. I firmly believe if you have some experienced in programming you can learn the basics of Python in a few days.

Python is easy to learn. For beginning programmers, Python is a great place to start. Learning to write simple programs is pretty easy, yet Python also scales up to complex "enterprise" systems. Python also scales with age, I have personally seen people from 7-80+ learn basic programming skills using Python.

Python is in demand. Python is widely used, and appears to be gaining popularity, especially among smaller startups. Back when I learned Python, we needed to hide that we were using it. Luckily those days are far behind us. Python is now found all over the wild workplaces of today, and is one of the most common languages found in startups.

Chapter 2

Which Version of Python?

This book will focus on Python 2. Python 3, has been out for a bit now and is somewhat backwards incompatible with the 2 series. Why use Python 2 then? Frankly for beginning Python, there are few differences. The current advantage of Python 2 is that third party library support is better. Every major library for Python is satisfied with version 2 yet some still do not feel much pressure to migrate to version 3.

For the most part, the examples in this book will run on both Python 2 and 3, but it was written and tested with Python 2 in mind. Which version of Python 2 does the book focus on? The examples were tested in 2.6 and 2.7 but should work in 2.4 and above.

2.1 Python installation

Python 2 is installed on many non-Windows platforms. If you are running on Mac or Linux you can skip the next paragraph.

For Windows folks, go to the download area of the Python website* and find a link that says "Python 2.7.5 Windows Installer" (2.7.5 was the most recent 2.7 version at the time of writing). This will link to a .msi file that will install python on your Windows machine. Download the file, and open it by double clicking it, and follow the instructions to finish the installation.

---

*http://www.python.org/download

2.2 Which editor?

In addition to installing Python, you will need a text editor. An editor is a tool for writing code. A skilled craftsman will invest the time to learn to use their tool appropriately and it will pay dividends. Learning to use the features of an editor can make churning out code easier. Many modern editors today have some semblance of support for Python. Note that Notepad and word processors are not really text editors, though they might act as such on Halloween. For Windows users, Notepad++ and the latest version of Visual Studio have Python support. For Mac people, Sublime Text appears to be a popular choice (note that this is also cross-platform). Kate and gedit are sensible Linux choices.

If you are just beginning with Python and have not had much experience with real text editors, most Python installations include IDLE. IDLE has decent Python editing features. The IDLE development environment also runs on Windows, Mac and Linux.

Many programmers favor Vim or Emacs. For Java people, both Eclipse (via PyDev) and JetBrains (via PyCharm) provide Python support. Wing is another cross platform Python specific editor that many favor. As mentioned previously, Sublime Text is another cross-platform editor that is gaining momentum. There are many other editors available, though one advantage of those mentioned in this paragraph is that they are cross platform if you find yourself working in different environments.

As you can tell there are many editors, and each has their advantages and disadvantages. If you do not have a favorite editing tool, it is probably best to use a simple one such as Notepad++, Sublime Text, or gedit. Editors such as Vim and Emacs have a slightly steeper learning curve, though their adherents would argue that it pays off to learn them well.

Chapter 3

The Interpreter

Python is commonly classified as an *interpreted* language. Another term used to describe an interpreted language is *scripting* language. In order to get computer programs to "run" on the CPU, the program must be in a format that the CPU understands, namely *machine code*. Interpreted languages do not *compile* directly to machine code, instead there is a layer above, an *interpreter* that performs this function.

There are pros and cons to this approach. As you can imagine, on the fly translating can be time consuming. Interpreted code like Python programs tend to run on the order of 10–100 times slower than C programs. On the flip side, writing code in Python optimizes for developer time. It is not uncommon for a Python program to be 2–10 times shorter than its C equivalent. Also, a compilation step can be time consuming and actually a distraction during development and debugging.

Many developers are willing to accept this trade-off. Smaller programs (read less lines of code) take less time to write and are easier to debug. Programmers can be expensive—if you can throw hardware at a problem, it can be cheaper than hiring more programmers. Debugging 10 lines of code is normally easier than debugging 100 lines of code. Studies have shown that the number of bugs found in code is proportional to the numbers of lines of code. Hence, if a language permits you to write fewer lines of code to achieve a given task, you will likely have fewer bugs. Sometimes program execution speed is not that important and Python is sufficiently fast for many applications. In addition there are efforts to improve the speed of Python interpreters such as PyPy[†].

3.1 Interactive interpreter

Because Python has an interpreter, this enables what is known as an *interactive interpreter* or *REPL* (Read Evaluate Print Loop). This is a loop that waits for input, evaluates it (interprets it), and prints out results. When you run the python executable by itself, you launch the interactive interpreter in Python. Other environments, such as IDLE, also embed an interactive interpreter.

3.2 A REPL example

Here is an example to illustrate where the read, evaluate, print, and loop come from:

```
$ python
>>> 2 + 2
4
>>>
```

In the above example, python was typed which opened the interpreter. The first >>> could be thought of as the *read* portion. Python is waiting for input. 2 + 2 is typed in, read, and *evaluated*. The result of that expression—4—is *printed*. The second >>> illustrates the *loop*, because the interpreter is waiting for more input.

The REPL, by default, prints any non-None result of an expression to standard out. This behaviour is inconsistent with normal Python programs, where the print statement must be explicitly invoked. But it saves a few keystrokes when in the REPL.

[†]http://www.pypy.org

Note

The >>> prompt is only used on the first line of each input. If the statement typed into the REPL takes more than one line, the ... prompt follows:

```
>>> sum([1, 2, 3, 4, 5,
...   6, 7])
```

These prompts are defined in the sys module:

```
>>> import sys
>>> sys.ps1
'>>> '
>>> sys.ps2
'... '
```

The REPL ends up being quite handy. You can use the interactive interpreter to write small functions, to test out code samples, or even to function as a calculator. Many Python programmers actually keep an interactive interpreter running in a terminal while they are developing. To get a flavor of how easy this is, start the interpreter now. Normally you would invoke python on the command line to start the interpreter. Another option is to start idle (which is included in many Python installations.)

At this point, you are strongly encouraged to find a computer with Python installed and follow along. For tactile learners, typing out the code can help you overcome initial fears about programming. Rather than solely reading about code, you can actually code! Run to your nearest computer before proceeding.

When you start the interpreter you should see lines similar to this:

```
Python 2.6.6 (r266:84292, Feb 26 2011,
23:10:42) [GCC 4.3.4] on linux2 Type
"copyright", "credits" or "license()"
for more information.

    **********************************
    Personal firewall software may
    warn about the connection IDLE
```

```
makes to its subprocess using this
computer's internal loopback
interface. This connection is not
visible on any external interface
and no data is sent to or received
from the Internet.
*********************************
```

```
IDLE 2.6.6
>>>
```

The >>> is a *prompt*. That is where you type your program. Type print "hello world" after the >>> and hit the enter key. Make sure there are not any spaces or tabs before the word print. You should see this:

```
>>> print "hello world"
hello world
```

If you see this, congratulations, you are writing Python. Consider yourself inducted into the world of programming. You have just run a program—"hello world". Hello world is the canonical program that most people write when encountering a new language.

Note

Programming requires precision. If you were not careful in typing exactly print "hello world" you might have seen something like this:

```
>>> print "hello world
SyntaxError: EOL while scanning
string literal
```

Computers are logical, and if your logic does not make sense, the computer can warn you, perform irrationally (or at least what appears so to you), or just die. Do not take it personally, but remember that languages have rules, and any code you write has to follow those rules. In the previous example, the rules that states if you want to print text on the screen you need to start and end the text with quotes was violated. A missing quote on the end of the line consequently confused Python.

Chapter 4

Running Programs

While using the interactive interpreter can be useful during development, most of the time you (and others) will want to *run* your deployed program outside of the REPL. In Python this is easy as well. To run a Python program named `hello.py`, simply open a terminal, go to the directory containing that program and type:

```
$ python hello.py
```

> **Note**
>
> When running a command from the command line, this book will precede the command with a $. This will distinguish it from interpreter contents (>>> or . . .) and file contents (nothing preceding the content).

> **Note**
>
> The previous command, `python hello.py`, will probably fail unless you have a file named `hello.py`.

In the previous chapter you just used the REPL to run "hello world", how does one run the same program standalone? Create a file named `hello.py` using your favorite text editor.

In your `hello.py` file type:

```
print "hello world"
```

Save the file, go to its directory, and *execute* the file (here *execute* and *run* have the same meaning, ie type `python` before the file name, and let the Python interpreter evaluate the code for you.)

> **Note**
>
> Typing `python` standalone launches the interpreter. Typing `python some_file.py` executes that file.

If you were successful at running `hello.py`, it would print out `hello world`.

4.1 Unixy embellishments

On Unix platforms (Linux and OS X among others), files such as `hello.py` are often referred to as *scripts*. A script is a program, but the term is often used to distinguish native code from interpreted code. In this case scripts are interpreted code, whereas the output from the compilation step of a language that compiles to machine code (such as C) is *native code*.

> **Note**
>
> It is not uncommon to hear about shell scripts, Perl scripts, Python scripts, etc. What is the difference between a Python script and a Python program? Nothing, really it is only semantics. A Python script usually refers to a Python program run from the command line, whereas a Python program is any program written in Python (which run the gamut of small 1-liners to fancy GUI applications, to "enterprise" class services).

Unix environments provide a handy way to make your script executable on it is own. By putting a *hash bang* (#!) on the first line of the file, followed by the path to the interpreter, and by changing the *executable bit* on the file, you can create a file that can run itself.

To tell have the script execute with the Python interpreter found in the environment, update your hello.py file to:

```
#!/usr/bin/env python
print "hello world"
```

Note

This new first line tells the shell that executes the file to run the rest of the file with the #!/usr/bin/env python executable. (Shell scripts usually start with #!/bin/bash or #!/bin/sh.) Save hello.py with the new initial line.

Tip

#!/usr/bin/env is a handy way to indicate that the first python executable found on your PATH environment variable should be used. Because the python executable is located in different places on different platforms, this solution turns out to be cross platform. Note that Windows ignores this line. Unless you are absolutely certain that you want to run a specific Python version, you should probably use #!/usr/bin/env.

Using hardcoded hashbangs such as:

- #!/bin/python

- #!/usr/bin/python2.4

Might work fine on your machine, but could lead to problems when you try to share your code and others do not have python where you specified it. If you require a specific version of Python, it is common to specify that in the README file.

Now you need to make the file executable. Open a terminal, cd to the directory containing hello.py and make the file executable by typing:

```
$ chmod +x hello.py
```

This sets the *executable bit* on the file. The Unix environment has different permissions (set by flipping a corresponding bit) for reading, writing, and executing a file. If the executable bit is set, the Unix environment will look at the first line and execute it accordingly, when the file is run.

Tip

If you are interested in knowing what the chmod command does, use the man (manual) command to find out by typing:

```
$ man chmod
```

Now you can execute the file by typing its name in the terminal and hitting enter. Type:

```
$ ./hello.py
```

And your program (or script) should run. Note the ./ included before the name of the program. Normally when you type a command into the terminal, the environment looks for an executable in the PATH (an environment variable that defines directories where executables reside). Unless . (or the parent directory of hello.py) is in your PATH variable you need to include ./ before the name (or the full path to the executable). Otherwise you will get a message like this:

```
$ hello.py
bash: hello.py command not found
```

Yes, all that work just to avoid typing python hello.py. Why? The main reason is that perhaps you want your program to be named hello (without the trailing .py). And perhaps you want the program on your PATH so you can run it at anytime. By making a file executable, and adding a hashbang, you can create a file that looks like an ordinary executable.

The file will not require a `.py` extension, nor will it need to be explicitly executed with the `python` command.

Chapter 5

Writing and Reading Data

Programs usually have some notion of input and output. For simple programs, printing values to the screen and allowing the end user to type in a value is usually sufficient. In Python both of these are really straightforward.

5.1 Simple output

The easiest way to provide the user with output is to use the `print` statement, which writes to *standard out*:

```
>>> print 'Hello there'
Hello there
```

> **Note**
>
> The above example illustrates typing `print` into the Python interpreter shell. In that case the interpreter will immediately execute the request, in this case printing `Hello there`.
>
> Printing from the interpreter is common. Seasoned programmers will keep an interpreter open during coding and use it as a scratch pad. If you follow along with the examples in this book, you will likely do many of them from the interpreter too.

Note

Part of the cleanup effort of Python 3 was to make the language more consistent. As a result `print` is a function in Python 3. Functions require parentheses to be invoked:

```
>>> print('Hello there')
Hello there
```

5.2 Getting user input

For basic input from the command line, Python includes the `raw_input` function. This function will print text out to the screen and wait until the user types something on *standard in* and hits enter:

```
>>> name = raw_input('Enter your name:')
```

If you typed in the above into the interpreter, it might look like your computer is frozen. In reality, it is waiting for you to type in some input. After you type something in and press enter, the variable `name` will hold the value you typed. Type the name `Matt` and press the enter key. If you print `name` it will print the value you just typed:

```
>>> print name
Matt
```

Note

The value entered for `raw_input` is always a *string*. If you want to convert it to another type like an integer or float, you will need to use the `int` and `float` functions respectively:

```
>>> value = raw_input('Enter a number:')
3
>>> value = int(value)
```

Note

In Python 3 raw_input is removed and input replaces it:

```
>>> value = input('Enter a number:')
```

Chapter 6

Variables

Now that you know about running programs via the interpreter (or the REPL) and the command line, it is time to start learning about programming. *Variables* are a basic building blocks of computer programs.

6.1 Mutation and state

Two important programming concepts are *state* and *mutation*. *State* deals with a digital representation of a model. For example, if you want to model a light bulb you may want to store its current status—is it on or off? Other possibly interesting states you could store include the type of bulb (CFL or incandescent), wattage, size, dimmable, etc.

Mutation deals with changing the state to a new or different state. For the light bulb example it could be useful to have a power switch that toggles the state.

Once you have objects that hold state and are mutable, then you have opened a world of possibilities. You can model most anything you want if you can determine what state it needs, and what actions or mutations need to apply to it.

6.2 Python variables are like tags

Variables are the building blocks of keeping track of state. You might think of a variable as a label or tag. Important information is tagged with a variable name. To continue the light bulb example, suppose that you want to remember the state of your light bulb. Having that data is only useful if you have access to it. If we want to access it and keep track of its state you need to have a *variable* to tag that data. Here the state of the bulb is stored in a variable named `status`:

```
>>> status = "off"
```

This requires a little more examination because there is a bit going on there. Starting from the right, there is the word `"off"` surrounded by quotes. The quotes tell Python that this object is a *string*. A string stores textual data—in this case the letters `off`. The = sign is the *assignment operator* in many programming languages. Do not be afraid of these technical terms, they are more benign than they appear. The assignment operator binds together a variable name and its state. It indicates that the name on the left of it is a variable that will hold object on the right. In this case the variable name is `status`.

Just to drive the point home, read it again from the left this time. `status` is a variable that is assigned to the string holding the state of `"off"`.

6.3   Cattle tags

My grandfather had a cattle ranch, so I will pull out a non-nerdy analogy. If you have a cattle ranch of any size it makes sense to have a good foreman who will keep track of your cattle (your investment). Note: that not all foreman take care of cattle and that cattle might mysteriously disappear or migrate to Mexico right under the nose of your foreman if you are not careful.

One way to keep track of cattle is to use cattle tags. These small tags attached to the ear of a cow can be used to identify and track individual cows.

In this example you are not running a cattle ranch, rather you are managing aspects of your program. A program can can hold many distinct pieces of information that you want to remember or keep track of. This information will is the *state*. For example if you needed to track data pertinent to humans you might want to track age, address, and name.

Just like how ranchers tags their cattle to keep track of them, programmers create variables to keep track of data. Cow tags (for those who have not ventured out to the country) are usually plastic tags that have a unique number on them and are attached semi-permanently to the cattle, normally to its ear. Look at the example again:

```
>>> status = "off"
```

This tells Python to create a *string* with the contents of off. Create a variable named status, and attach it to that string. Later on when you need to know what the status is, you can ask your program to print it out like so:

```
>>> print status
off
```

It is entirely possible to create *state* and lose it to the ether if you neglect to put it in a variable. It is somewhat useless to create objects that you would not use, but again it is possible. Suppose you want to keep track of the bulb's wattage. If you write:

```
>>> "120 watt"
```

It tells Python to create an string object with the content of 120 watt. But you have got a problem now, because you forgot to assign it to a variable. Now, you have no way of using it. Python will only let you access data that is stored in variables, so it is impossible for you to use this item now. Objects are accessed by using their variable names. If this was information that you needed in your program, a better solution would be the following:

```
>>> wattage = "120 watt"
```

Later on in your program you can access wattage, you can print it out, and you can even assign another variable to it, or assign wattage to another new value (say if your incandescent bulb broke and you replaced it with an LED bulb):

```
>>> incandescent = wattage
```

```
>>> wattage = "25 watt"
>>> print incandescent, wattage
120 watt 25 watt
```

Managing state is a core aspect of programming. Variables are one mechanism to manage it.

Chapter 7

Basic Types

The last chapter discussed variables for storing *string* objects. Strings in and of themselves are quite useful, but often it makes sense to represent other types of state. There are many types of *objects* built into Python that come in handy. If these built-in types are not sufficient to model what you need, you can even define your own objects—*classes*.

7.1 *Strings*

A *string* holds character information that can have any number of characters (including 0):

```
>>> name = 'Matt'
>>> with_quote = "I ain't gonna"
>>> longer = """This string has
... multiple lines
... in it"""
>>> latin = '''Lorum ipsum
... dolor'''
>>> escaped = 'I ain\'t gonna'
>>> zero_chars = ''
```

Strings are specified with single quotes, double quotes or triple quotes. The triple version (which can consist of double or single quotes) is useful because it allows the string to span multiple lines. It is important though to ensure that the ending quotes match the initial quotes. Also note that single quoted strings can contain double quotes in them and vice-versa. However if you want to include a single quote in a single quoted string you must *escape* the inner quotes by preceding them with a backslash \.

7.2 *Integers* and *floats*

An *integer* is a whole number. Whole numbers are numbers like 3, 0, or -10. A *float* represents real numbers. Real numbers have decimal places in them like 2.5, 0.0, or -5.0 (note that the content following a # is a comment and ignored by Python):

```
>>> a = 4    # integer
>>> b = 5.6  # float
```

Python's floats are represented internally using a binary representation (as per the IEEE 754 standard for floating point numbers). As such, they lack precision and rounding errors are possible. In fact one should expect rounding errors. (If you need precision, the `decimal` module provides a more precise albeit slower implementation). As a quick example, examine what happens when you perform this apparently simple subtraction operation:

```
>>> print 1.01 - .99
0.0200000000000000018
```

> **Tip**
>
> If you are interested in understanding more about how computers represent floats, wikipedia has probably more information than you would want on the subject. Just search for the term "Floating point".

7.3 *Booleans*

Booleans are a built-in type to represent a binary toggle between true and false. Booleans are frequently used to keep track of the status of a task, ie whether it is done or not. You could use a boolean to keep track of whether you have cleaned your room. Here are the variable c is set to the boolean that represents true, which the d variable is set to the boolean that represents false:

```
>>> c = True
>>> d = False          .
```

7.4 Rebinding variables

Much like cow tags, variables tend to stay with an object for a while, but they are transferable. Python lets you easily change the variable:

```
>>> a = 4
>>> a = '4'   # now a is a string
```

In the above example a was holding an integer, but then held a string. There is no limit to how often you can change a variable. But you should be careful not to change a variable if you still need access to the old data. Once you remove all variables from an object, you are essentially telling Python to destroy (*garbage collect* is the proper geeky term) the object when it has the chance, to free up any internal memory it occupies.

7.5 Naming variables

There is only one rule enforced by Python about naming variables: *Variables should not be a keyword*. The word break is a keyword and hence cannot be used as a variable:

```
>>> break = 'foo'
  File "<stdin>", line 1
    break = 'foo'
         ^
SyntaxError: invalid syntax
```

> **Note**
>
> Keywords are reserved for use in Python language constructs, so it confuses Python if you try to make them variables.

Note (cont.)

The module keyword has a kwlist attribute, that is a list containing all the current keywords for Python:

```
>>> import keyword
>>> print keyword.kwlist
['and', 'as', 'assert', 'break',
'class', 'continue', 'def', 'del',
'elif', 'else', 'except', 'exec',
'finally', 'for', 'from', 'global',
'if', 'import', 'in', 'is',
'lambda', 'not', 'or', 'pass',
'print', 'raise', 'return', 'try',
'while', 'with', 'yield']
```

7.6   Additional naming considerations

In addition to the aforementioned rule about not naming variable after keywords, there are a few best practices encouraged by the Python community. The rules are simple—variables should:

- be lowercase

- use an underscore to separate words

- not start with numbers

- not override a *built-in* function

Here are examples of variable names, both good and bad:

```
>>> good = 4
>>> bAd = 5  # bad - capital letters
>>> a_longer_variable = 6

# this style is frowned upon
>>> badLongerVariable = 7

# bad - starts with a number
>>> 3rd_bad_variable = 8
  File "<stdin>", line 1
    3rd_bad_variable = 8
```

```
# bad - keyword
>>> for = 4
  File "<stdin>", line 1
    for = 4
        ^
SyntaxError: invalid syntax

# bad -  built-in function
>>> compile = 5
```

> **Tip**
>
> Rules and conventions for naming in Python come from a document named "PEP 8 – Style Guide for Python Code". PEP stands for Python Enhancement Proposal, which is a community process for documenting a feature, enhancement or best practice for Python. PEP documents are found on the Python website.

> **Note**
>
> Although Python will not allow keywords as variable names, it will allow you to use a *built-in* name as a variable. Built-ins are functions, classes or variables that Python automatically preloads for you, so you get easy access to them. Unlike keywords, Python will let you use a built-in as a variable name without so much as a peep. However, you should refrain from doing this, it is a bad practice.
>
> Using a built-in name as a variable name *shadows* the built-in. The new variable name prevents you from getting access to the original built-in. Essentially you took the built-in variable and co-opted it for your use. To get access to the original built-in you will need to access it through the __builtin__ module. But it is much better not to shadow it in the first place.
>
> Here is a list of Python's *built-ins* that you should avoid using as variables:

29

Note (cont.)

```
>>> import __builtin__
>>> dir(__builtin__)
['ArithmeticError',
'AssertionError', 'AttributeError',
'BaseException', 'BufferError',
'BytesWarning',
'DeprecationWarning', 'EOFError',
'Ellipsis', 'EnvironmentError',
'Exception', 'False',
'FloatingPointError',
'FutureWarning', 'GeneratorExit',
'IOError', 'ImportError',
'ImportWarning', 'IndentationError',
'IndexError', 'KeyError',
'KeyboardInterrupt', 'LookupError',
'MemoryError', 'NameError', 'None',
'NotImplemented',
'NotImplementedError', 'OSError',
'OverflowError',
'PendingDeprecationWarning',
'ReferenceError', 'RuntimeError',
'RuntimeWarning', 'StandardError',
'StopIteration', 'SyntaxError',
'SyntaxWarning', 'SystemError',
'SystemExit', 'TabError', 'True',
'TypeError', 'UnboundLocalError',
'UnicodeDecodeError',
'UnicodeEncodeError',
'UnicodeError',
'UnicodeTranslateError',
'UnicodeWarning', 'UserWarning',
'ValueError', 'Warning',
'ZeroDivisionError', '_',
'__debug__', '__doc__',
'__import__', '__name__',
'__package__', 'abs', 'all', 'any',
'apply', 'basestring', 'bin',
'bool', 'buffer', 'bytearray',
'bytes', 'callable', 'chr',
'classmethod', 'cmp', 'coerce',
'compile', 'complex', 'copyright',
'credits', 'delattr', 'dict', 'dir',
'divmod', 'enumerate', 'eval',
'execfile', 'exit', 'file',
'filter', 'float', 'format',
'frozenset', 'getattr', 'globals',
```

Note (cont.)

```
'hasattr', 'hash', 'help', 'hex',
'id', 'input', 'int', 'intern',
'isinstance', 'issubclass', 'iter',
'len', 'license', 'list', 'locals',
'long', 'map', 'max', 'min', 'next',
'object', 'oct', 'open', 'ord',
'pow', 'print', 'property', 'quit',
'range', 'raw_input', 'reduce',
'reload', 'repr', 'reversed',
'round', 'set', 'setattr', 'slice',
'sorted', 'staticmethod', 'str',
'sum', 'super', 'tuple', 'type',
'unichr', 'unicode', 'vars',
'xrange', 'zip']
```

Note

In Python3 the __builtin__ module is renamed to builtins.

Tip

Here are built-ins that would be good variable names otherwise:

- dict

- file

- id

- list

- open

- str

- sum

- type

Chapter 8

More about objects

This chapter will dive into objects a little bit more. You will cover three important properties of objects:

- identity

- type

- value

8.1 Identity

Identity at its lowest level refers to the location in the computer's memory of an object. Python has a built-in function—id that tells you the identity of an object:

```
>>> name = "Matt"
>>> id(name)
140310794682416
```

When you type this, the identity of the string "Matt" will appear as 140310794682416 (which refers to a location in the RAM of your computer). This will generally vary for each computer and for each time you start the shell, but the id of an object is consistent across the lifetime of a program.

Do note that just as it is possible for a single cow to have two tags on its ears, it is also possible for two variables to refer to the same object. Hence, running id on either of the two variables will return the same id. If you want another variable—first—to also refer to the same object referred to by name, you could do the following:

```
>>> first = name
```

This tells Python to give the first variable the same id of name. Later you could use the is operator to validate that they are actually the same:

```
>>> first is name
True
>>> id(first)
140310794682416
```

If you print either first or name at the REPL, it will print the same value because they pointing to the exact same value:

```
>>> print first
Matt
>>> print name
Matt
```

8.2   Type

Another property of an object is its *type*. Common types are *strings*, *integers*, *floats*, and *booleans*. There are many other kinds of types, and you can create your own as well. The type of an object refers to the class of an object. A class defines the *state* of data an object holds, and the *methods* or actions that it can perform. Python allows you to easily view the type of an object with the build-in function type:

```
>>> type(name)
<type 'str'>
```

The type function tells you that the variable name holds a string (str).

The table below shows the types for various obejcts in Python.

Object	Type
String	`str`
Integer	`int`
Floating point	`float`
List	`list`
Dictionary	`dict`
Tuple	`tuple`
function	`function`
User defined class[‡]	`classobj`
Instance of User defined class[§]	`instance`
User defined class (subclass object)	`type`
Instance of class (subclass of class)	`class`
built-in function	`builtin_function _or_method`
type	`type`

Due to *duck-typing* the type function is somewhat frowned upon. Python provides built-in classes, `str`, `int`, `float`, `list`, `dict`, and `tuple` that convert (or coerce) to the appropriate type if needed:

```
>>> str(0)
'0'

>>> tuple([1,2])
(1, 2)

>>> list('abc')
['a', 'b', 'c']
```

[‡]Python 2 only.

[§]Python 2 only.

8.3 Mutability

A final interesting property of an object is its *mutability*. Many objects are *mutable* while others are *immutable*. *Mutable* objects can change their value in place, in other words you can alter their state, but their *identity* stays the same. Objects that are *immutable* do not allow you to change their value. Instead you can change their variable reference to a new object, but this will change the *identity* variable to the new object as well.

In Python, *dictionaries* and *lists* are *mutable* types. *Strings*, *tuples*, *integers*, and *floats* are *immutable* types. Here is an example demonstrating that the identity of a variable holding an integer will change if you change the value:

```
>>> age = 10
>>> id(age)
140310794682416
>>> age = age + 1
>>> id(age)
140310793921824   # DIFFERENT!
```

Here is an example of changing a list. Note that even after we add an item to the list, the identity of the list is unchanged:

```
>>> names = []
>>> id(name)
140310794682432
>>> names.append("Fred")
>>> id(name)
140310794682432   # SAME!
```

Mutable objects should not be used for keys in dictionaries and can present problems when used as default parameters for functions.

Chapter 9

Numbers

This chapter will discuss manipulating numbers with Python. *Integers* (whole numbers like -1, 5, or 2000) and *Floating Points* (the computer's approximation of real numbers like .333, 0.5 or -1000.234) are available in Python and allow for easy numerical manipulation. Out of the box, Python provides support for addition, subtraction, multiplication, division, power, modulo, and more!

Unlike other languages, in Python everything is an object, including numbers. Integers are of class `int` or `long`:

```
>>> type(1)
<type 'int'>
```

Floating point numbers are of class `float`:

```
>>> type(2.0)
<type 'float'>
```

9.1 Addition

The Python REPL can also be used as a simple calculator. If you want to add two integers it is easily done:

```
>>> 2 + 6
8
```

Note that adding two integers together results in an integer.

Likewise you can also add two floats together:

```
>>> .25 + 0.2
0.45000000000000001
```

This example illustrates once again that care is needed when using floating point numbers, as you can lose precision (the real result would be 0.45).

What happens when you add an integer and a float?

```
>>> 6 + .2
6.2000000000000002
```

Aha, Python decided that because you are adding an integer and a float, you need floating point arithmetic. In this case Python converts, or *coerces*, 6 to a float behind the scenes, before adding it to .2. Python has given you the answer back as a float (note again, the slightly incorrect answer).

Note

If you have an operation involving two numerics, coercion generally does the right thing. For operations involving an integer and a float, the integer is coerced to a float. If both numerics are floats or integers, no coercion takes place. The function coerce is a built-in that illustrates numeric coercion. It takes two arguments and returns a tuple with numeric coercion applied:

```
>>> coerce(2, 2.)
(2.0, 2.0)
>>> coerce(2, 2)
(2, 2)
>>> coerce(2., 2.)
(2.0, 2.0)
```

Note

Coercion between strings and numerics does not occur with most mathematical operations. The exception being the string formatting operator, %, if the left operand is a string:

Note (cont.)

```
>>> coerce('2', 2)
Traceback (most recent call last):
  File "<stdin>", line 1, in <module>
Type Error: number coercion failed
>>> print 'num: %s' % 2
num: 2
```

Note

Explicit conversion can be done with the int and float built-in classes. (Note that they look like functions but are really classes):

```
>>> int(2.3)
2
>>> float(3)
3.0
```

9.2 Subtraction

Subtraction is similar to addition. Subtraction of two integers or two floats returns an integer or a float respectively. For mixed numeric types, the operands are coerced before performing subtraction:

```
>>> 2 - 6
-4
>>> .25 - 0.2
0.049999999999999989
>>> 6 - .2
5.7999999999999998
```

9.3 Multiplication

In many programming languages the * (asterisk) is used for multiplication. You can probably guess what is going to happen when you multiply two integers:

```
>>> 6 * 2
12
```

If you have been following carefully, you will also know what happens when you multiply two floats:

```
>>> .25 * 12.0
3.0
```

And if you mix the types of the product you end up with a float as a result:

```
>>> 4 * .3
1.2
```

Note that the float result in these examples appears correct, though you should be careful not to assume that you would always be so lucky.

9.4 Division

In Python (like many languages) the / symbol is used for division. What happens when the operation is applied to the different types? Start with integers:

```
>>> 12 / 4
3
```

Good, integer division returns integers. Are you seeing a pattern yet? Not so quick though, what happens when you do the following?

```
>>> 3 / 4
0
```

That might not be what you expected. Three divided by four is .75, yet Python claims it is zero. This is a gotcha, known as *integer division*. In Python, when you divide integers, the result is going to be an integer. What integer does Python use? The *floor* of the real result—take the answer and round down.

> **Note**
>
> This is considered such a heinous wart that in Python 3, the / operator automatically coerces the operands to floats before performing the operation. Hence, the answer will be a float. If you really want *integer division* in Python 3, you need to use the // (double slash) operator.

If you want a slightly more precise answer you need to coerce one of the numbers (either the numerator or the divisor) to a float:

```
>>> 3 / 4.0
0.75
>>> 3.0 / 4
0.75
```

In the above example one of the numbers was manually changed to a float (ie typed 4.0 instead of 4). How would you do that programmatically? Luckily Python gives you a way to do that using the built-in float class:

```
>>> numerator = 3
>>> float(numerator)
3.0

>>> numerator / 4
0
>>> float(numerator) / 4
0.75
```

The float class takes an *argument* (numerator in the example above) and returns an object that holds a floating point number. float will also try and convert other types to float if it can. For example if you have a variable holding a *string* that looks like a number, you can coerce it using float:

```
>>> number = "3"
>>> float(number)
3.0
```

If your string does not really look like a number though, Python will complain:

```
>>> float('Matt')
Traceback (most recent call last):
  File "<stdin>", line 1, in <module>
ValueError: invalid literal for
float(): Matt
```

> **Note**
>
> The built-in class, int, will coerce variables into integers if it can:
>
> ```
> >>> int('2')
> 2
> >>> int(2.2)
> 2
> ```

9.5 Modulo

The *modulo* operator (%) calculates the remainder in a division operation. This is useful for determining whether a number is odd or even (or whether you have just iterated over 1000 items):

```
# remainder of 4 divided by 3
>>> 4 % 3
1
```

> **Tip**
>
> Be careful with the modulo operator and negative numbers. Modulo can behave differently, depending on which operand is negative. It makes sense that if you are counting down, the modulo should cycle at some interval:
>
> ```
> >>> 3 % 3
> 0
> >>> 2 % 3
> 2
> >>> 1 % 3
> 1
> ```

Tip (cont.)

```
>>> 0 % 3
0
```

What should -1 % 3 be? Since you are counting down it should cycle over to 2 again:

```
>>> -1 % 3
2
```

But when you switch the sign of the denominator, the behavior becomes weird:

```
>>> -1 % -3
-1
```

Python guarantees that the sign of the modulo result is the same as the denominator (or zero). To further confuse you:

```
>>> 1 % -3
-2
```

The take away here is that you probably do not want to do modulo with negative numbers on the denominator unless you are sure that is what you need.

9.6 Power

Python also gives you the *power* operator by using the ** (double asterisks). If you wanted to square 4, the following will do it:

```
>>> 4 ** 2
16
```

Exponential growth tends to let numbers get large pretty quickly. Consider raising 10 to the 100th power:

```
>>> 10 ** 100
10000000000000000000000000000000000000000
00000000000000000000000000000000000000000
00000000000000000000000000L
```

If you look carefully at the result, after the 100 zero's, there is an L. The L stands for *Long* (or long integer). Programs need to use a certain amount of memory to store integers. Because integers are usually smaller numbers, Python optimizes for them, to not waste memory.

An analogy might be a scale. If you are always weighing small amounts, you might want a small scale. If you deal in sand you will probably want to put the sand in a bag to make it easier to handle. You will have a bunch of small bags that you will use. But if you occasionally need to weigh larger items that do not fit on the small scale, you need to pull out a bigger scale, and a bigger bag. It would be a waste to use the bigger bag and scale for many of the smaller items.

Similarly, Python tries to optimize storage space for integers towards smaller sizes. When Python does not have enough memory (a small bag) to fit larger integers in, it *coerces* the integer into a *long integer*. This is actually desireable, because in some environments, you run into an *overflow error* here, where the program dies (or Pac-Man refuses to go over level 255—since it stored the level counter in an 8 bit number).

> **Note**
>
> Python will tell you at what point it considers a number an *integer* or a *long integer*. In the sys module there is a variable, `maxint` that defines this. On my computer (a 64-bit computer) this number is:
>
> ```
> >>> import sys
> >>> sys.maxint
> 9223372036854775807
> ```
>
> (It just so happens that this number is (2 ** 64)/2 - 1. For the mathematically inclined, 64 bits are used to represent an integer. Python can represent whole numbers from 0 to 2 ** 64 -1. But because integers also deal with negative numbers, computers use half of the space to represent negatives (hence the /2). On a 32 bit computer it would be a bit smaller. This representation of integers is named *two's complement*)

Note (cont.)

Once you get larger than this value, you get *longs* as the result of integer number manipulation. (Note the L):

```
>>> sys.maxint + 1
9223372036854775808L
```

Tip

Why not always work with *longs* if they can represent more numbers? In practice, you do not need them because Python will do the right thing. (Unless you are counting on integer overflow). The main reason is performance, longs are slower to work with (bigger bags/more memory). Unless you need longs, stay away so as to not incur a performance penalty. If you feel an urge to use longs, the class long will coerce to a long, much like int or float.

In Python 3, there is no long type because the details of how the number is represented by the computer is completelly handled behind the scenes.

Note

Python includes the operator module that has functions for the common mathematical operations. When using more advanced features of Python such as lambda functions or *list comprehensions*, these come in handy:

```
>>> import operator
>>> operator.add(2, 4)  # same as 2 + 4
6
```

9.7   Order of operations

Usually when you are performing math, you do not just apply all the operations from left to right. You do multiplication and division before addition and subtraction. Computers work the same way. If you want to perform addition (or subtraction) first, use parentheses to indicate the order of operations:

```
>>> 4 + 2 * 3
10
>>> (4 + 2) * 3
18
```

As illustrated in the example, anything in parentheses is evaluated first.

Chapter 10

Strings

Strings are objects that hold character data. A string could hold a single character, a word, a line of words, a paragraph, multiple paragraphs or even zero characters.

Python denotes strings by wrapping them with ' (single quotes), " (double quotes), """ (triple doubles) or ' ' ' (triple singles). Here are some examples:

```
>>> character = 'a'
>>> word = "Hello"

>>> line = "ain't"

>>> print line
ain't
```

Notice that the strings always start and end with the same style of quote. As illustrated in the line example you can put double quotes inside of a single quoted string—and vice versa. Furthermore, if you need to include the same type of quote within your string, you can *escape* the quote by preceding it with a \ (backslash). When you print out an escaped character the backslash is ignored.

> **Note**
>
> Attentive readers may wonder how to include a backslash in a string. To include a backslash in a nor-

Note (cont.)

mal string, you must escape the backslash with ... you
guessed it, another backslash:

```
>>> backslash = '\\'
>>> print backslash
\
```

Note

Here are the common escape sequences in Python:

Escape Sequence	Output
\\	Backslash
\'	Single quote
\"	Double quote
\b	ASCII Backspace
\n	Newline
\t	Tab
\u12af	Unicode 16 bit
\U12af89bc	Unicode 32 bit
\o84	Octal character
\xFF	Hex character

Tip

If you do not want to use an escape sequence, you
can make a *raw* string, by preceding the string with an r.
Raw strings are normally used in regular expressions,
where the backslash can be common.

Raw strings interpret the character content literally
(ie. there is no escaping). The following illustrates the
difference between raw and normal strings:

```
>>> slash_t = r'\tText \\'
>>> print slash_t
\tText \\
```

Python also includes the triple quoting mechanism for defining strings. This is useful for creating strings containing paragraphs or multiple lines. Triple quoted strings are also commonly used in *docstrings*. Docstrings will be discussed in the chapter on functions. Here is an example of a multi-line triple quoted string:

```
>>> paragraph = """Lorem ipsum dolor
... sit amet, consectetur adipisicing
... elit, sed do eiusmod tempor incididunt
... ut labore et dolore magna aliqua. Ut
... enimad minim veniam, quis nostrud
... exercitation ullamco laboris nisi ut
... aliquip ex ea commodo consequat. Duis
... aute irure dolor in reprehenderit in
... voluptate velit esse cillum dolore eu
... fugiat nulla pariatur. Excepteur sint
... occaecat cupidatat non proident, sunt
... in culpa qui officia deserunt mollit
... anim id est laborum."""
```

Chapter 11

Formatting Strings

Storing strings in variables is nice, but being able to compose strings of other strings and manipulate them is also necessary. One way to achieve this is to use string formatting.

In Python 2.6 and above (including 3.x), the preferred way to format strings is to use the `format` method of strings. Here is an example:

```
>>> name = 'Matt'
>>> print 'Hello {0}'.format(name)
Hello Matt
```

When a string contains curly braces ({ and }) with an integer inside it, the braces serve as a placeholder for the variable passed into `format`. In this case you are telling Python to replace {0} with the contents of `name` or the string `Matt`.

Another useful property of formatting is that you can also format non-string objects, such as numbers:

```
>>> print 'I:{0} R:{1} S:{2}'.format(1, 2.5, 'foo')
I:1 R:2.5 S:foo
```

If you are paying careful attention, you will note that the numbers in the curly braces are incrementing. In reality they tell the format operation which object to insert and where. Many computer languages start counting from 0, so {0} would correspond with the integer 1, and the {1} would be 2.5, while the {2} is the string 'foo'.

11.1 Format string syntax

Format strings have a special syntax for *replacement fields*. In the previous examples integers were used to represent positional argument locations. If an object is passed into the format string attributes can be looked up used .attribute_name syntax. There is also support for pulling index-able items out by using [index] as well:

```
>>> 'Name: {0}'.format('Paul')
'Name: Paul'

>>> 'Name: {name}'.format(name='John')
'Name: John'

>>> 'Name: {[name]}'.format({'name':'George'})
'Name: George'
```

There is a whole language for formatting strings. The form is:

```
:[[fill]align][sign][#][0][width][,][.precision][type]
```

The following tables lists the fields and their meaning.

Field	Meaning
fill	Fills in space with align
align	<-left align, >-right align, ^-center align, =-put padding after sign
sign	+-for all number, --only negative, *space*-leading space for positive, sign on negative
#	Prefix integers. 0b-binary, 0o-octal, 0x-hex
0	Enable zero padding
width	Minimum field width
,	Use comma for thousands separator
.precision	Digits after period (floats). Max string length (non-numerics)
type	s-string format (default) see Integer and Float charts

Integer Types	Meaning
b	binary
c	character - convert to unicode character
d	decimal (default)
n	decimal with locale specific separators
o	octal
x	hex (lower-case)
X	hex (upper-case)

Float Types	Meaning
e/E	Exponent. Lower/upper-case e
f	Fixed point
g/G	General. Fixed with exponent for large, and small numbers (g default)
n	g with locale specific separators
%	Percentage (multiplies by 100)

11.2 format **examples**

Format a string in the center of 12 characters surrounded by *:

```
>>> "Name: {0:*^12}".format("Ringo")
'Name: ***Ringo****'
```

Format a percentage using a width of 10, one decimal place and the sign before the width padding:

```
>>> "Percent: {0:=10.1%}".format(-44./100)
'Percent: -    44.0%'
```

Binary and hex conversions:

```
>>> "Binary: {0:b}".format(12)
'Binary: 1100'

>>> "Hex: {0:x}".format(12)
'Hex: c'
```

Note

The format method on a string replaces the % operator which was similar to C's printf. This operator is still available and some users prefer it because it requires less typing for simple statements and because it is similar to C. %s, %d, and %x are replaced by their string, integer, and hex value respectively. Here are some examples:

```
>>> "Num: %d Hex: %x" % (12, 13)
'Num: 12 Hex: d'

>>> "%s %s" % ('hello', 'world')
'hello world'
```

Chapter 12

dir, help, and pdb

You have only just touched the surface of strings, but you need to take a break to discuss two important functions and one library that are built-in to Python. The first function is dir, which illustrates wonderfully how powerful and useful the REPL is. The dir function indicates the attributes of an object. If you had a Python interpreter open and wanted to know what the attributes of a string are, you can do the following:

```
>>> dir('Matt')
['__add__', '__class__',
'__contains__', '__delattr__',
'__doc__', '__eq__', '__format__',
'__ge__', '__getattribute__',
'__getitem__', '__getnewargs__',
'__getslice__', '__gt__', '__hash__',
'__init__', '__le__', '__len__',
'__lt__', '__mod__', '__mul__',
'__ne__', '__new__', '__reduce__',
'__reduce_ex__', '__repr__',
'__rmod__', '__rmul__', '__setattr__',
'__sizeof__', '__str__',
'__subclasshook__',
'_formatter_field_name_split',
'_formatter_parser', 'capitalize',
'center', 'count', 'decode', 'encode',
'endswith', 'expandtabs', 'find',
'format', 'index', 'isalnum',
'isalpha', 'isdigit', 'islower',
'isspace', 'istitle', 'isupper',
```

```
'join', 'ljust', 'lower', 'lstrip',
'partition', 'replace', 'rfind',
'rindex', 'rjust', 'rpartition',
'rsplit', 'rstrip', 'split',
'splitlines', 'startswith', 'strip',
'swapcase', 'title', 'translate',
'upper', 'zfill']
```

dir lists all the attributes of the object passed into it. Since you passed in the string 'Matt' to dir, the function displays the attributes of the string Matt. This handy feature of Python illustrates its "batteries included" philosophy. Python gives you an easy mechanism to discover the attributes of any object. Other languages might require special websites, documentation or IDE's to access similar functionality. But in Python, because you have the REPL, you can get at this information quickly and easily.

The attribute list is in alphabetical order, and you can normally ignore the first couple of attributes starting with __. Later on you will see attributes such as capitalize (which is a *method* that capitalizes a string), format (which as you illustrated, allows for formatting of strings), or lower (which is a *method* used to ensure the string is lowercase). These attributes happen to be *methods*, which are easy to invoke on a string:

```
>>> print 'matt'.capitalize()
Matt
>>> print 'Hi {0}'.format('there')
Hi there
>>> print 'YIKES'.lower()
yikes
```

12.1   Dunder methods

You might be wondering what all the attributes starting with __ are. People call them *magic methods* or *dunder* methods, since they start (and end) with double underscores (Double UNDERscores). "Dunder add" is one way to say __add__, "the add magic method" is another. Special methods determine what happens under the covers when operations are performed on an object. For example when you use the + or /

operator on a string, the __add__ or __div__ method is invoked respectively.

Beginner Pythonistas can usually ignore dunder methods. When you start implementing your own classes and want them to react to operations such as + or / you can define them.

12.2 help

help is another built-in function that is useful in combination with the REPL. This function provides documentation for methods, modules, classes, and functions (if the documentation exists). For example, if you are curious what the attribute upper on a string does, the following gives you the documentation:

```
>>> help('some string'.upper)
Help on built-in function upper:

upper(...)
    S.upper() -> string

    Return a copy of the string S
    converted to uppercase.
```

12.3 pdb

Python includes a debugger to step through code named pdb. This library is modeled somewhat after the gdb library for C. To drop into the debugger at any point a Python program, insert the code import pdb; pdb.set_trace(). When this line is executed it will present a (pdb) prompt, which is similar to the REPL. Code can be evaluated and inspected live. Also breakpoints can be set and further inspection can take place.

Below is a table listing useful pdb commands:

Command	Purpose
h, help	List the commands available
n, next	Execute the next line
c, cont, continue	Continue execution until a breakpoint is hit
w, where, bt	Print a stack track showing where execution is
u, up	Pop up a level in the stack
d, down	Push down a level in the stack
l, list	List source code around current line

Note

Many Python developers use *print debugging*. They insert print statements to provide clarity as to what is going on. This is often sufficient. Just make sure to remove the debug statements or change them to logging statements before releasing the code. When more exploration is required, the pdb module can be useful.

Chapter 13

Strings and methods

In the previous chapter you learned about the built-in `dir` function and saw some methods you can call on string objects. Strings allow you to `capitalize` them, `format` them, make them lowercase (`lower`), as well as many other actions. These attributes of strings are *methods*. *Methods* are functions that are called on an instance of a type. Try to parse out that last sentence a little. The string type allows you to *call* a method (another term for call is *invoke*) by placing a . (period) and the method name directly after the variable name holding the data (or the data itself), followed by parentheses with arguments inside of them.

Here is an example of calling the `capitalize` method on a string:

```
>>> name = 'matt'

# invoked on variable
>>> correct = name.capitalize()
>>> print correct
Matt

# invoked on data
>>> print 'fred'.capitalize()
Fred
```

In Python methods and functions are *first-class objects*. If the parentheses are left off, Python will not throw an error, it will simply show a reference to a method:

```
>>> print 'fred'.capitalize
<built-in method capitalize of str object at
0x7ff648617508>
```

This is a feature that comes in handy and enables more advanced features like *closures* and *decorators*.

Note

Do integers and floats have methods? Yes, all types in Python are classes, and classes have methods. This is easy to verify by invoking `dir` on an integer (or a variable holding an integer):

```
>>> dir(4)
['__abs__', '__add__', '__and__',
 '__class__',
 ...
 '__subclasshook__', '__truediv__',
 '__trunc__', '__xor__', 'conjugate',
 'denominator', 'imag', 'numerator',
 'real']
```

Invoking a method on a number is somewhat tricky due to the use of the . to denote calling a method. Because . is common in floats, it would confuse Python if . were also used to call methods on numbers.

For example, the conjugate method returns the complex conjugate of any integer. But if you try to invoke it on an integer, you will get an error:

```
>>> 5.conjugate()
File "<stdin>", line 1
  5.conjugate()
            ^
SyntaxError: invalid syntax
```

One solution to this is to wrap the number with parentheses:

```
>>> (5).conjugate()
5
```

Another option would be to assign a variable to 5 and invoke the method on the variable:

Note (cont.)

```
>>> five = 5
>>> five.conjugate()
5
```

However, it is fairly rare to call methods on numbers.

13.1 Common string methods

Here are a few string methods that are commonly used or found in the wild. Feel free to explore others using `dir` and `help` (or the online documentation).

13.2 endswith

If you have a variable holding a filename, you might want to check the extension. This is easy with `endswith`:

```
>>> xl = 'Oct2000.xls'
>>> xl.endswith('.xls')
True
>>> xl.endswith('.xlsx')
False
```

Note

Notice that you had to pass in a *parameter*, `'xls'`, into the method. Methods have a *signature*, which is a funky way of saying that they need to be called with the correct number (and type) of parameters. For `endswith` it makes sense that if you want to know if a string ends with another string you have tell Python which ending you want to check for. This is done by passing the end string to the method.

61

Tip

Again, it is usually easy to find out this sort of information via help. The documentation should tell you what parameters are required as well as any optional parameters. Here is the help for endswith:

```
>>> help(xl.endswith)
Help on built-in function endswith:

endswith(...)
    S.endswith(suffix[, start[, end]]) -> bool

    Return True if S ends with the specified
    suffix, False otherwise. With optional
    start, test S beginning at that position.
    With optional end, stop comparing S at
    that position. suffix can also be a
    tuple of strings to try.
```

Notice the line S.endswith(suffix[, start[, end]]) -> bool. The S represents the string you are invoking the method on, in this case the xl variable. .endswith is the method name. Between the parentheses, (and), are the parameters. suffix is a *required* parameter, the endswith method will complain if you do not provide it:

```
>>> xl.endswith()
Traceback (most recent call last):
  File "<stdin>", line 1, in
  <module>
TypeError: endswith() takes at
least 1 argument (0 given)
```

The parameters between the square brackets [and] are *optional* parameters. In this case start and end allow you to only check a portion of the string. If you wanted to check if the characters starting at 0 and ending at 3 end with Oct you could do the following:

```
>>> xl.endswith('Oct', 0,3)
True
```

13.3 find

The find method allows you to find substrings inside other strings. It returns the *index* (offset starting at 0) of the matched substring. If no substring is found it returns -1:

```
>>> word = 'grateful'

# 0 is g, 1 is r, 2 is a
>>> word.find('ate')
2
>>> word.find('great')
-1
```

13.4 format

format allows for easy creation of new strings by combining existing variables. The variables replace {X} (where X is an integer):

```
>>> print 'name: {0}, age: {1}'.\
... format('Matt', 10)
name: Matt, age: 10
```

> **Note**
>
> In the above example, the print statement is spread across two lines. By placing a \ following a . you indicate to Python that you want to continue on the next line. If you have opened a left parenthesis, (, you can also place the arguments on multiple lines without a \:
>
> ```
> >>> print "word".\
> ... find('ord')
> 1
> >>> print "word".find(
> ... 'ord')
> 1
> ```
>
> Note that indenting with four spaces serves to indicate to anyone reading the code that the second line is a continuation of a previous statement:

Note (cont.)

```
>>> print "word".\
...     find('ord')
1
>>> print "word".find(
...     'ord')
1
```

Why spread code that could reside in a single line across multiple lines? Where this comes into play in most code is dealing with code standards that expect lines to be less that 80 characters in length. If a method takes multiple arguments, it may be hard to follow the 80 character limit. (Note that Python itself does not care about line length, but readers of your code might). It is not uncommon to see a separate line for each argument to a method:

```
>>> print '{0} {1} {2} {3} {4}'.format(
...     'hello',
...     'to',
...     'you',
...     'and',
...     'you'
... )
hello to you and you
```

13.5 join

join creates a new string from a sequence by inserting a string between every member of the list:

```
>>> ', '.join(['1','2','3'])
'1, 2, 3'
```

Tip

For most Python interpreters, using join is faster than repeated concatenation using the + operator. The above idiom is common.

13.6 startswith

startswith is analogous to endswith except that it checks
that a string starts with another string:

```
>>> 'Book'.startswith('B')
True
>>> 'Book'.startswith('b')
False
```

13.7 strip

strip removes preceding and trailing *whitespace* (spaces, tabs,
newlines) from a string. This may come in handy if you have
to normalize data or parse input from a user (or the web):

```
>>> '   hello   there   '.strip()
'hello   there'
```

Note that three spaces at the front of the string were removed as were the two at the end. But the two spaces between
the words were left intact. If you are interested in removing
only the leading whitespace or rightmost whitespace, the
methods lstrip and rstrip respectively will perform those
duties.

There are other string methods, but they are used less
often. Feel free to explore them by reading the documentation
and trying them out.

Chapter 14

Comments, Booleans, and
None

14.1 Comments

Comments are not a type per se, because they are ignored by Python. Comments serve as reminders to the programmer. There are various takes on comments, their purpose, and their utility. Opinions vary about comments. There is a continuum of those who are against any and all comments, those who comment almost every line of code, and those who are in between. If you are contributing to a project, try to be consistent with their commenting scheme. A basic rule of thumb is that a comment should explain the *why* rather than the *how* (code alone should be sufficient for the how).

To create a comment in Python simply start a line with a #:

```
>>> # This line is ingored by Python
```

You can also comment at the end of a line:

```
>>> num = 3.14  # PI
```

> **Tip**
>
> A rogue use of comments is to temporarily disable code during editing. If your editor supports this, it is sometimes easier to comment out code rather than remove it completely. But the common practice is to remove commented-out code before sharing the code with others.

Other languages support multi-line comments, but Python does not. The only way to comment multiple lines is to start every line with #.

> **Tip**
>
> You may be tempted to comment out multiple lines of code by making those lines a triple quoted string. This is ugly and confusing. Try not to do this.

14.2 Booleans

Booleans represent the true and false values. You have already seen them in previous code examples, such as the result of .startswith:

```
>>> a = True
>>> b = False
>>> 'bar'.startswith('b')
True
```

> **Note**
>
> The actual name of the boolean class in Python is *bool*.
>
> ```
> >>> type(True)
> <type 'bool'>
> ```

It can be useful convert other types to booleans. In Python, the bool class can do that. Converting from one type to another is called *casting*. This is usually unnecessary due to implicit casting Python when conditionals have an object. It is common to hear in Python parlance of objects behaving as "truthy" or "falsey"—that just means that non-boolean types can implicitly behave as though they were booleans. If you are unsure what the behavior might be, pass in the type to the bool class for an explicit conversion (or cast).

Note

For the built-in types, int, float, str, and bool, even though they are capitalized as if they were functions, they are classes. Invoking help(str) will confirm this:

```
>>> help(str)
class str(basestring)
 |   str(object) -> string
 |
 |   Return a nice string representation of
 |   the object. If the argument is a string,
 ...
```

For numbers, zero coerces to False while other numbers have "truthy" behavior:

```
>>> bool(0)
False
>>> bool(4)
True
```

For strings, an empty string is "falsey", while non-empty coerce to True:

```
>>> bool('')
False
>>> bool('0')  # The string containing 0
True
```

While explicit casting via the bool function is available, it is usually overkill, because variables are implicitly coerced to booleans when used in conditional statements. For example, container types, such *lists* and *dictionaries*, when empty, behave as "falsey". On the flipside, when they are populated they act as "truthy".

> **Tip**
>
> Be careful when parsing content that you want to turn into booleans. Strings that are non-empty evaluate to True. One example of a string that might bite you is the string 'False' which evaluates to True:
>
> ```
> >>> bool('False')
> True
> ```

Here is a table of truthy and falsey values:

Truthy	*Falsey*
True	False
Most objects	None
1	0
3.2	0.0
[1, 2]	[] (empty list)
{'a': 1, 'b': 2}	{} (empty dict)
'string'	"" (empty string)
'False'	
'0'	

> **Tip**
>
> Do not test boolean values to see if they are equal to True. If you have a variable, done, containing a boolean, this is sufficient:
>
> ```
> >>> if done:
> ...     # do something
> ```
>
> While this is overkill:
>
> ```
> >>> if done == True:
> ...     # do something
> ```

Tip (cont.)

Similarly if you have a list and need to distinguish between an empty and non-empty list, this is sufficient:

```
>>> members = []
>>> if members:
...     # do something if members
...     # have values
... else:
...     # member is empty
```

Likewise this test is superfluous. It is not necessary to determine the truthiness of a list by its length:

```
>>> if len(members):
...     # do something if members
...     # have values
... else:
...     # member is empty
```

Note

If you wish to define the implicit truthiness for self defined objects, the __nonzero__ method specifies this behavior. It can return True, or False. If this magic method is not defined, the __len__ method is checked for a non-zero value. If neither method is defined, an object defaults to True.

14.3 None

None is a special type in Python—NoneType. Other languages have similar constructs such as *NULL* or *undefined*. Variables can be assigned to None to indicate that they are waiting to hold a real value. None coerces to False in a boolean context:

```
>>> bool(None)
False
```

Note

A Python function defaults to returning None if no return statement is specified.

Note

None is a *singleton* (Python only has one copy of None in the interpreter):

```
>>> a = None
>>> id(a)
140575303591440
>>> b = None
>>> id(b)
140575303591440
```

As any variable containing None is the same object as any other variable containing None, it is common to use is to check for *identity* with these variables rather than using == to check for *equality*:

```
>>> a is b
True
>>> a is not b
False
```

Chapter 15

Conditionals and whitespace

In addition to the boolean type in Python, you can also use expressions to get boolean values. For comparing numbers, it is common to check if they are greater than or less than other numbers. > and < do this respectively:

```
>>> 5 > 9
False
```

Here is a table of expressions to create boolean constructs:

Check	Meaning
>	Greater than
<	Less than
>=	Greater than or equal to
<=	Less than or equal to
==	Equal to
!=	Not equal to
is	Identical object
is not	Not identical object

These expressions work on most types, or custom classes that define the appropriate magic methods:

```
>>> name = 'Matt'
>>> name == 'Matt'
True
```

```
>>> name != 'Fred'
True
>>> 1 > 3
False
```

Note

The "rich comparison" magic methods, __gt__, __lt__, __ge__, __le__, _eq__, and __ne__ correspond to >, <, >=, <=, ==, and != respectively. For classes where these comparisons are commonly used, the functools.total_ordering class decorator allows for only defining __eq__ and __le__. The decorator will automatically derive the remainder of the comparison methods. Otherwise all six methods should be implemented:

```
>>> import functools
>>> @functools.total_ordering
>>> class Abs(object):
...     def __init__(self, num):
...         self.num = abs(num)
...     def __eq__(self, other):
...         return self.num == abs(other)
...     def __lt__(self, other):
...         return self.num < abs(other)

>>> five = Abs(-5)
>>> four = Abs(-4)
>>> five > four  # not using less than!
True
```

Tip

is and is not are for comparing *identity*. When testing for identity—if two objects are the same actual object (not just have the same value)—use is or is not. Since None is a singleton and only has one identity, is and is not are used with None:

```
>>> if name is None:
...     # initialize name
```

15.1 Combining conditionals

Conditional expressions can be combined using *boolean logic*. This logic consists of the and, or, and not operators.

Boolean Operator	Meaning
x and y	Both x and y must evaluate to True for true result
x or y	If x or y is True, result is true
not x	Negate the value of x (True becomes False and vice versa)

Here is a simple example for checking a grade using and:

```
>>> score = 91
>>> if score > 90 and score <= 100:
...     grade = 'A'
```

Here is an example for checking if a given name is a member of a band:

```
>>> name = 'Paul'
>>> beatle = False
>>> if name == 'George' or \
...     name == 'Ringo' or \
...     name == 'John' or \
...     name == 'Paul':
...     beatle = True
... else:
...     beatle = False
```

> **Note**
>
> In the above example the \ following 'George' or indicates that the statement will be continued on the next line.
>
> Like most programming languages, Python allows you to wrap conditional statements in parentheses. Because they are not required in Python, most developers leave them out unless they are needed for operator precedence. But another subtlety of using parentheses

> **Note (cont.)**
>
> is that they serve as a hint to the interpreter when a statement is still open and will be continued on the next line, hence the \ is not needed in that case:
>
> ```
> >>> name = 'Paul'
> >>> beatle = False
> >>> if (name == 'George' or
> ...     name == 'Ringo' or
> ...     name == 'John' or
> ...     name == 'Paul'):
> ...     beatle = True
> ... else:
> ...     beatle = False
> ```

Here is an example of using the not keyword in a conditional statement:

```
>>> last_name = 'unknown'
>>> if name == 'Paul' and not beatle:
...     last_name = 'Revere'
```

15.2 if **statements**

Booleans (True and False) are often used in *conditional* statements. Conditional statements are instructions that say "if this statement is true, do that, otherwise do something else." This is a useful construct and is used frequently in Python. Sometimes the "if statement" will check values that contain booleans, other times it will check *expressions* that evaluate to booleans. Another common check is for implicit coercion to "truthy" or "falsey" values:

```
>>> debug = True
>>> if debug:  # checking a boolean
...     print "Debugging"
Debugging
```

15.3 else **statements**

Here is an example of adding an else statement and expressions that evaluate to booleans. This is for a school that has grade inflation:

```
>>> score = 87
>>> if score >= 90:
...     grade = 'A'
... else:
...     grade = 'B'
```

Note that the *expression*, score >= 90, is evaluated by Python and turns into a False. Because the "if statement" was false, the statements under the else block are executed, and the grade variable is set to 'B'.

15.4 **More choices**

The previous example does not work for most schools. You can add more intermediate steps if needed using the elif keyword. elif is an abbreviation for "else if". Here is a more complete grading example:

```
>>> score = 87
>>> if score >= 90:
...     grade = 'A'
... elif score >= 80:
...     grade = 'B'
... elif score >= 70:
...     grade = 'C'
... elif score >= 60:
...     grade = 'D'
... else:
...     grade = 'F'
```

Note

The if statement can have zero or more elif statements, but they can only have up to one else statements.

> **Note**
>
> Note that after the `if` and `elif` statements come their blocks. The block following a conditional statement is only executed when its conditional statement evaluates to `True`, or when the `else` statement is encountered.

15.5 Whitespace

Another peculiarity you may have noticed is the colon (`:`) following the boolean expression in the `if` statement. The lines immediately after were indented by four spaces. The indented lines are the *block* of code that is executed when the `if` expression evaluates to `True`.

In many other languages an `if` statement looks like this:

```
if (score >= 90) {
    grade = 'A';
}
```

In many of these languages the curly braces { and } denote the if block. Any code between these braces is executed when the score is greater than or equal to 90.

Python, unlike those other languages, uses two things to denote blocks:

- a colon (`:`)

- indentation

If you have programmed in other languages, it is easy to convert to Python, by replacing the left curly bracket ({) with a colon (`:`) and indenting consistently until the end of the block.

> **Tip**
>
> What is consistent indentation? Normally either tabs or spaces are used to indent code. In Python four spaces is the preferred way to indent code. This is described in

Tip (cont.)

PEP 8 . If you mix tabs and spaces you will eventually run into problems.

Although spaces are the preferred mechanism, if you are working on code that already uses tabs, it is better to be consistent. In that case continue using tabs with the code.

The python executable also has a -tt command line option that will cause any inconsistent usage of spaces and tabs to throw errors.

Chapter 16

Sequences: Lists, tuples, and sets

Many of the types discussed so far have been *scalars*, which hold a single value. Integers, floats, and booleans are all scalar values.

Sequences hold collections of objects (scalar types or even other sequences). This chapter will discuss collections—lists, tuples and sets.

16.1 Lists

Lists, as the name implies, are used to hold a list of objects. They are a *mutable type*, meaning you can add, remove, and alter the contents of them. There are two ways to create empty lists, one is with the list function, and the other is using the square bracket literal syntax—[and]:

```
>>> names = list()
>>> other_names = []
```

If you want to have prepopulated lists, you can provide the values in between the square brackets, using the *literal syntax*:

```
>>> other_names = ['Fred', 'Charles']
```

> **Note**
>
> The list function can also create prepopulated lists, but it is somewhat redundant because you have to pass a list into it:
>
> ```
> >>> other_names = list(['Fred', 'Charles'])
> ```

Lists, like other types, have methods that you can call on them (use dir([]) to see a complete list of them). To add items to the end of a list use the append method:

```
>>> names.append('Matt')
>>> names.append('Fred')
>>> print names
['Matt', 'Fred']
```

16.2   Sequence indices

To work effectively with sequences it is important to understand what an *index* is. Every item in a list has an associated index, which describes its location in the list. For example the ingredients in potato chips are potatoes, oil, and salt, and they are normally listed in that order. Potatoes are first in the list, oil is second and salt is third. In many programming languages, the first item in a sequence is at index 0, the second item is at index 1, the third at index 2, and so on. Counting beginning with zero is call *zero-based indexing*.

You can access an item in a list using the bracket notation and the index of said item:

```
>>> print names[0]
Matt

>>> print names[1]
Fred
```

16.3 List insertion

If you want to insert an item at a certain *index*, use the insert method. Calling insert will shift any items following that index to the right:

```
>>> names.insert(0, 'George')
>>> print names
['George', 'Matt', 'Fred']
```

The syntax for replacement at an index is the bracket notation:

```
>>> names[1] = 'Henry'
>>> print names
['George', 'Henry', 'Fred']
```

To append items to the end of a list use the append method:

```
>>> names.append('Paul')
>>> print names
['George', 'Henry', 'Fred', 'Paul']
```

> **Note**
>
> CPython's underlying implementation of a list is actually an array of pointers. This provides quick random access to indices. Also appending/removing at the end of a list is quick (O(1)), while inserting/removing from the middle of a list is slower (O(n)). If you find yourself inserting and popping from the front of a list, a collections.deque might be a better data structure.

16.4 List deletion

To remove an item use the remove method:

```
>>> names.remove('Paul')
>>> print names
['George', 'Henry', 'Fred']
```

As with many of the other operations on lists, you can also delete by index using the bracket notation:

```
>>> del names[1]
>>> print names
['George', 'Fred']
```

16.5 Sorting lists

Another common operation on lists is *sorting*. Sorting is done with the sort method. This method sorts the list *in place*. It does not return a new, sorted copy of the list:

```
>>> names.sort()
>>> print names
['Fred', 'George']
```

If the previous order of the list was important, you can make a copy of it before sorting. Another option is to use the sorted function. sorted creates a new list that is reordered:

```
>>> old = [5, 3, -2, 1]
>>> nums_sorted = sorted(old)
>>> print nums_sorted
[-2, 1, 3, 5]
>>> print old
[5, 3, -2, 1]
```

By default, Python sorts *lexically*. You can think of this as alphabetical sorting. But it might be confusing if you are not used to it. For example, integers come before numbers in strings when sorting them, and uppercase letters are treated as distinct from their lowercase partners:

```
>>> things = [2, 'abc', 'Zebra', '1']
>>> things.sort()
>>> print things
[2, '1', 'Zebra', 'abc']
```

Both the sort method and sorted function allow arbitrary control of sorting by passing in a function for the key parameter. In this example, by passing in str as the key parameter, every item in the list is sorted as if it were a string:

```
>>> things.sort(key=str)
>>> print things
['1', 2, 'Zebra', 'abc']
```

The key parameter can be any callable (function, class, method) that takes a single item and returns something that can be compared.

> **Note**
>
> In Python 2, sort and sorted also accept a cmp parameter. This is removed from Python 3. key can provide the same functionality and is slightly faster.

16.6 Useful list hints

As usual, there are other methods found on lists. Do not hesitate to open the Python interpreter and type a few examples. Remember that dir and help are your friends.

> **Tip**
>
> The Python built-in function range constructs integer lists. If you needed the numbers zero through four, you can easily get it with range:
>
> ```
> # numbers < 5
> >>> nums = range(5)
> >>> print nums
> [0, 1, 2, 3, 4]
> ```
>
> Notice that range does not include 5 in its list. Many Python functions dealing with final indices mean "up to but not including". (Slices are another example of this you will see later).
>
> If you need to start at a non-zero number, range can take two parameters as well. When there are two parameters, the first is the starting number (including it), and the second is the "up to but not including" number:
>
> ```
> # numbers from 2 to 5
> >>> nums2 = range(2, 6)
> >>> print nums2
> [2, 3, 4, 5]
> ```

Tip (cont.)

range also has an optional third parameter—*stride*. A stride of one (which is the default) means the next number in the sequence range returns should be one more than the previous. A stride of 2 would return every other number. This is an easy way to get only even numbers:

```
>>> even = range(0, 11, 2)
>>> print even
[0, 2, 4, 6, 8, 10]
```

Note

The "up to but not including" construct is also more formally known as the *half-open interval* convention. It is commonly used when defining sequences of natural numbers. This has a few nice properties:

- The diffence between the end and start is the length when dealing with a sequence of subsequent numbers

- Two subsequences can be spliced together cleanly without overlap

Python adopts this idiom widely. If you are dealing with numeric sequences you might want to follow suit, especially when defining api's.

16.7   Tuples

Tuples (commonly pronounced as either "two"-ples or "tuh"-ples) are *immutable* sequences. Once you create them, you cannot change them. Similar to the list square bracket *literal sytax*, there is a parentheses literal syntax for tuples. There is also a tuple function that you can use to construct a new tuple from an existing list or tuple:

```
>>> b = (2,3)
>>> print b
(2, 3)

>>> c = tuple([2,3])
>>> print c
(2, 3)
```

There are two ways to create an empty tuple, using the tuple function or parentheses:

```
>>> empty = tuple()
>>> print empty
()

>>> empty = ()
>>> print empty
()
```

Here are three ways to create a tuple with one item in it:

```
>>> one = tuple([1])
>>> print one
(1,)

>>> one = (1,)
>>> print one
(1,)

>>> one = 1,
>>> print one
(1,)
```

Note

   Because parentheses are used for both denoting the calling of functions or methods in Python as well as tuple creation, this can lead to confusion. Here's the simple rule, if there is one item in the parentheses, then Python treats the parentheses as normal parentheses (for operator precedence), such as those that you might use when writing (2 + 3) * 8. If there is more than one item in the parentheses, then Python treats it as a tuple:

```
>>> d = (3)
```

Note (cont.)

```
>>> type(d)
<type 'int'>
```

In the above example, d might look like a tuple with parentheses but Python claims it is an integer. For tuples with only one item, it is necessary in Python to put a comma (,) following the item—or use the tuple function with a single item list:

```
>>> e = (3,)
>>> type(e)
<type 'tuple'>
```

Here are three ways to create a tuple with more than one item:

```
>>> many = tuple([1,2,3])
>>> print many
(1, 2, 3)

>>> many = (1,2,3)
>>> print many
(1, 2, 3)

>>> many = 1,2,3
>>> print many
(1, 2, 3)
```

Because tuples are immutable you cannot append to them:

```
>>> c.append(4)
Traceback (most recent call last):
  File "<stdin>", line 1, in <module>
AttributeError: 'tuple' object has no attribute
'append'
```

Note

Why the distinction between tuples and lists? Why not use lists since they appear to be a super-set of tuples?

The main difference is mutability. Because tuples are immutable they are able to serve as keys in dictionaries.

> **Note (cont.)**
>
> Tuples are often used to represent a record of data such
> as the results of a database query, which may contain
> heterogeneous types of objects. Perhaps a tuple would
> contain a name, address, and age:
>
> ```
> >>> person = ('Matt', '123 North 456 East', 24)
> ```
>
> Tuples are used for returning multiple items from
> a function. Tuples also serve as a hint to the developer
> that this type is not meant to be modified.

16.8 Sets

Another sequence type found in Python is a *set*. A set is an
unordered sequence that cannot contain duplicates. Like a
tuple it can be instantiated with a list. There are a few differences. First, unlike lists and tuples, a set does not care about
order. Also, unlike a tuple or list, there is no special sytax to
create sets, you have to call the set class (another coercion
class that appears as a function). Pass the set class a list, and
it will create a sequence with any duplicates removed:

```
>>> digits = [0, 1, 1, 2, 3, 4, 5, 6,
... 7, 8, 9]

# remove extra 1
>>> digit_set = set(digits)
>>> digit_set
set([0, 1, 2, 3, 4, 5, 6, 7, 8, 9])
```

Sets are useful because they allow for *set operations*, such
as union (|), intersection (&), difference (-), and xor (^) among
two sets.

Difference (-) allows you to remove items in one set from
another:

```
>>> odd = set([1, 3, 5, 7, 9])

# difference
>>> even = digit_set - odd
>>> print even
```

```
set([0, 8, 2, 4, 6])
```

Notice that the order of the result is somewhat arbitrary at a casual glance. If order is important, a set is not the data type you should use.

Intersection (&) is an operation that returns the items found in both sets:

```
>>> prime = set([2, 3, 5, 7])

# those in both
>>> prime_even = prime & even
>>> print prime_even
set([2])
```

The *union* (|) operation returns a set composed of both sets, with duplicates removed:

```
>>> numbers = odd | even
>>> print numbers
set([0, 1, 2, 3, 4, 5, 6, 7, 8, 9])
```

Xor (^) is an operation that returns a set of items that only are found in one set or the other, but not both:

```
>>> first_five = set([0, 1, 2, 3, 4])
>>> two_to_six = set([2, 3, 4, 5, 6])
>>> in_one = first_five ^ two_to_six
>>> print in_one
set([0, 1, 5, 6])
```

Tip

Why use a set instead of a list? Sets are optimized for set operations. If you find yourself performing unions or differences among lists, look into using a set instead.

Sets are also quicker for testing membership. The in operator runs faster for sets than lists. However, this speed comes at a cost. Sets do not keep the elements in any particular order, whereas lists do.

Chapter 17

Iteration

A common idiom when dealing with sequences is to loop over the contents of the sequence. The for loop is the most common way to do this. Here is an example of printing out the numbers in a list:

```
>>> for number in [1, 2, 3, 4]:
...     print number
1
2
3
4
```

> **Note**
>
> Notice that a for loop construct contains a colon (:) followed by indented code. (The indented code is the *block* of the for loop).

17.1 Looping with an index

In many other languages, when you loop over a sequence, you do not loop over the items in the sequence, rather you loop over the indices. Using those indices you can pull out the items at those index values. Here is one way to do that in Python using the built-in functions range and len:

```
>>> animals = ["cat", "dog", "bird"]
>>> for index in range(len(animals)):
...     print index, animals[index]
0 cat
1 dog
2 bird
```

The above code is considered bad in Python. Usually you only need the items in the sequence. But occasionally you will also need the index position of the item. Python provides the built-in enumerate function that makes the combination of range and len unnecessary. The enumerate function returns a tuple of (index, item) for every item in the sequence:

```
>>> animals = ["cat", "dog", "bird"]
>>> for index, value in \
...     enumerate(animals):
...     print index, value
0 cat
1 dog
2 bird
```

17.2   Breaking out of a loop

You may need to stop processing a loop early, without going over every item in the loop. The break keyword will jump out of the nearest loop you are in. If you have a program that adds numbers until it comes to the first negative one, you could use break to stop when you hit a negative number:

```
>>> numbers = [3, 5, 9, -1, 3, 1]
>>> result = 0
>>> for item in numbers:
...     if item < 0:
...         break
...     result = result + item
>>> print result
17
```

> **Note**
>
> Note that the `if` block inside the `for` block is indented eight spaces. Blocks can be nested, and each level needs to be indented consistently.

17.3   Skipping over items in a loop

Another common looping idiom is to skip over items. If the body of the `for` loop takes a while to execute, but you only need to execute it for certain items in the sequence, the `continue` keyword comes in handy. The `continue` keyword tells Python to disregard processing of the current item in the for loop and "continue" from the top of the for block with the next value in the loop.

Here is an example of summing all positive numbers:

```
>>> numbers = [3, 5, 9, -1, 3, 1]
>>> result = 0
>>> for item in numbers:
...     if item < 0:
...         continue
...     result = result + item
>>> print result
21
```

17.4   Removing items from lists during iteration

It was mentioned previously that lists are mutable. Because they are mutable you can add or remove items from them. Also, because lists are sequences you can loop over them. It is advisable *not* to mutate the list at the same time that you are looping over it.

For example, if you wanted to filter a list of names so it only contained 'John' or 'Paul', this would be the wrong way to do it:

```
>>> names = ['John', 'Paul', 'George',
... 'Ringo']
```

93

```
>>> for name in names:
...     if name not in ['John', 'Paul']:
...         names.remove(name)

>>> print names
['John', 'Paul', 'Ringo']
```

What happened? Python assumes that lists will not be modified while they are being iterated over. Otherwise, the for loop will not cover every member of the list.

There are two alternative to the above contruct of removing items from a list during iteration. The first is to collect the items to be removed during a pass through the list. In a subsequent loop over only the items that need to be deleted (names_to_remove), remove them from the original list—names:

```
>>> names = ['John', 'Paul', 'George',
... 'Ringo']
>>> names_to_remove = []
>>> for name in names:
...     if name not in ['John', 'Paul']:
...         names_to_remove.append(name)

>>> for name in names_to_remove:
...     names.remove(name)

>>> print names
['John', 'Paul']
```

Another option is to iterate over a copy of the list. This can be done relatively painlessly using the [:] slice copy construct that is covered in the chapter on slicing:

```
>>> names = ['John', 'Paul', 'George',
... 'Ringo']
>>> for name in names[:]:   # copy of names
...     if name not in ['John', 'Paul']:
...         names.remove(name)

>>> print names
['John', 'Paul']
```

17.5   else **clauses**

A for loop can also have an else clause. Any code in an else
block will execute if the for loop did not hit a break statement.
Here is some sample code that checks if numbers in a loop
were positive:

```
>>> positive = False
>>> for num in items:
...     if num < 0:
...         break
... else:
...     positive = True
```

Note that continue statements do not have any effect on
whether an else block is executed.

Chapter 18

Dictionaries

Dictionaries store data by mapping keys to values. *Lists* also map keys to values, they map the index position to the value.

18.1 Dictionary assignment

Dictionaries map *keys* to *values*. (Other languages may call them *hashes*, *hash maps*, *maps*, or *associative arrays*). Suppose you had a collection of names and ages, it might be appropriate to use a dictionary to hold that information. The following allows for quick lookup of age by name:

```
>>> ages = {'Pete': 11}
>>> ages['George'] = 10
>>> ages['Fred'] = 12
>>> ages['Henry'] = 10
```

In the above example the keys are the names. For example 'George' is the *key* that maps to the integer 10, the *value*.

The above example illustrates the literal syntax for creating an initially populated dictionary. It also shows how the square brackets are used to insert items into a dictionary. They associate a key with a value, when used in combination with the *assignment operator* (=).

18.2 Retrieving values from a dictionary

The square bracket literal syntax also serve to pull a value
out of a dictionary when you use the brackets without assignment:

```
>>> print ages['George']
10
```

Be careful though, if you try to access a key that does not
exist in the dictionary, Python will throw an exception:

```
>>> print ages['Charles']
Traceback (most recent call last):
  File "<stdin>", line 1, in <module>
KeyError: 'Charles'
```

18.3 The in operator

Python provides an *operator*, in, that allows you to quickly
check if a key is in a dictionary:

```
>>> 'Matt' in ages
False
>>> 'Fred' in ages
True
```

> **Tip**
>
> Dictionaries also have a has_key method, that is similar to the in operator. Idiomatic Python favors in to
> has_key:
>
> ```
> >>> ages.has_key('Matt')
> False
> ```

18.4 Dictionary shortcuts

The get method of a dictionary will retrieve a value for a key.
get also accepts an optional parameter to provide a default

value if the key is not found. If you wanted the default age to be 1 you could do the following:

```
>>> chucks_age = ages.get('Charles', 1)
>>> print chucks_age
1
```

> **Tip**
>
> The get method of dictionaries is one way to get around the KeyError thrown when trying to use the bracket notation to pull out a key not found in the dictionary.

18.5 setdefault

A useful, but somewhat confusingly named, method of dictionaries is the setdefault method. The method has the same signature as get and initially behaves like it, returning a default value if the key does not exist. In addition to that, it also sets the value of the key to the default value if the key is not found. Because setdefault returns a value, if you initialize it to a mutable type, such as a dict or list, you can mutate the result in place.

setdefault can be used to provide an accumulator or counter for a key. For example if you wanted to count the number of people with same name, you could do the following:

```
>>> names = ['Ringo', 'Paul', 'John',
... 'Ringo']
>>> count = {}
>>> for name in names:
...     count.setdefault(name, 0)
...     count[name] += 1
```

Without setdefault you would have to use a bit more code:

```
>>> names = ['Ringo', 'Paul', 'John',
... 'Ringo']
>>> count = {}
```

```
>>> for name in names:
...     if name not in count:
...         count[name] = 1
...     else:
...         count[name] += 1
```

> **Tip**
>
> The collections.Counter class found in Python 2.7
> and Python 3 can perform the above operations much
> more succinctly:
>
> ```
> >>> import collections
> >>> count = collections.Counter(['Ringo', 'Paul',
> ...     'John', 'Ringo'])
> >>> count
> Counter({'Ringo': 2, 'Paul': 1, 'John': 1})
> >>> count['Ringo']
> 2
> >>> count['Fred']
> 0
> ```

Here is a somewhat contrived example illustrating mutating the result of setdefault. Assume you want to have a dictionary mapping names to bands. If a person named Paul is in two bands, the result should map Paul to a list containing both of those bands:

```
>>> band1_names = ['John', 'George',
... 'Paul', 'Ringo']
>>> band2_names = ['Paul']
>>> names_to_bands = {}
>>> for name in band1_names:
...     names_to_bands.setdefault(name,
...         []).append('Beatles')
>>> for name in band2_names:
...     names_to_bands.setdefault(name,
...         []).append('Wings')
>>> print names_to_bands['Paul']
['Beatles', 'Wings']
```

To belabor the point, without setdefault this code would be a bit longer:

```
>>> band1_names = ['John', 'George',
```

```
...   'Paul', 'Ringo']
>>> band2_names = ['Paul']
>>> names_to_bands = {}
>>> for name in band1_names:
...       if name not in names_to_bands:
...           names_to_bands[name] = []
...       names_to_bands[name].\
...           append('Beatles')
>>> for name in band2_names:
...       if name not in names_to_bands:
...           names_to_bands[name] = []
...       names_to_bands[name].\
...           append('Wings')
>>> print names_to_bands['Paul']
['Beatles', 'Wings']
```

Tip

The collections module from the Python standard library includes a handy class—defaultdict. This class behaves just like a dictionary but it also allows for setting the default value of a key to an arbitrary factory. If the default factory is not None, it is initialized and inserted as a value any time a key is missing.

The previous example re-written with defaultdict is the following:

```
>>> from collections import defaultdict
>>> names_to_bands = defaultdict(list)
>>> for name in band1_names:
...       names_to_bands[name].\
...           append('Beatles')
>>> for name in band2_names:
...       names_to_bands[name].\
...           append('Wings')
>>> print names_to_bands['Paul']
['Beatles', 'Wings']
```

Using defaultdict is slightly more readable than using setdefault.

18.6 Deleting keys

Another common operation on dictionaries is removal of keys and their corresponding values. To remove an item from a dictionary, simply use the del operator:

```
# remove 'Ringo' from dictionary
>>> del names_to_bands['Ringo']
```

> **Tip**
>
>   Like deletion from a list while iterating over it, be careful about removing keys from a dictionary while iterating over the same dictionary.

18.7 Dictionary iteration

Dictionaries also support iteration using the for statement. Because dictionaries are unordered, do not rely on a consistent order. By default a dictionary iterates over its keys:

```
>>> data = {'Adam': 2, 'Zeek': 5, 'Fred': 3}
>>> for name in data:
...     print name
Zeek
Adam
Fred
```

> **Note**
>
>   The dictionary has a method—keys—that will also list out the keys of a dictionary.

To iterate over the values of a dictionary, simply iterate over the values method:

```
>>> for value in data.values():
...     print value
5
2
3
```

To retrieve both key and value during iteration, use the
`items` method:

```
>>> for key, value in data.items():
...     print key, value
Zeek 5
Adam 2
Fred 3
```

> **Tip**
>
> If the order of iteration is important, either sort the
> sequence of iteration or use a data structure that stores
> order information.
>
> The built-in function `sorted` will return a new sorted
> list, given a sequence:
>
> ```
> >>> for name in sorted(data.keys()):
> ...     print name
> Adam
> Fred
> Zeek
> ```
>
> It also provides an optional argument, `reverse`, to
> flip the order of the output:
>
> ```
> >>> for name in sorted(data.keys(),
> ...     reverse=True):
> ...     print name
> Zeek
> Fred
> Adam
> ```

Chapter 19

Functions

You have come a long way without discussing functions, which are a basic building block of many Python programs. Functions are discrete units of code, isolated into their own block. You have actually been using built-in functions along the way such as dir, help, (and the classes that behave like coercion functions—float, int, long and bool).

One way to think of a function is as a black box that you can send input to (though input is not required). The black box then performs a series of operations and possibly returns some output.

Here is a simple example of a function. This function, named add_2 takes a number as input, adds 2 to that value and returns the result:

```
>>> def add_2(num):
...       '''
...       return 2 more than num
...       '''
...       result = num + 2
...       return result
```

What are the different components of a function? This whole group of code would be known as a *function definition*. First you see the def statement, which is short for *define* (ie define a function). Following def is a required space (one space is fine) and then the function name—add_2. This is the name that is used to *invoke* the function. Invoke is a nerdy way of saying execute the function. Following the function name is a left parenthesis followed by num and a right parenthesis. The names between the parentheses (there can be an arbitrary number of names, in this case there is only one), are the input *parameters*. These are the objects that you pass into a function.

After the parentheses comes a colon (:). Whenever you see a colon in Python, you should immediately think it is followed by an indented block. (This is similar to the body of the for loops shown previously.) Everything indented is the *body* of the function. It might also be referred to as a *block of code*.

The body of a function is where the logic lives. You might recognize the first 3 lines of indented code as a triple quoted string. Python allows you to place a string immediately after the : that contains a *docstring*. A docstring is a string used solely for documentation. It should describe the block of code following it. The docstring does not affect the logic in the function.

Tip

The help function has been emphasized through this book. It is important to note that the help function actually gets its content from the *docstring* of the object passed into it. If you call help on add_2, you should see the following (provided you actually typed out the add_2 code above):

```
>>> help(add_2)
Help on function add_2 in module
__main__:

add_2()
    return 2 more than num
(END)
```

Providing docstrings can be useful to you as a reminder of what your code does, but if they are accurate, they are invaluable to anyone trying to use your code.

Following the docstring (note that a docstring is optional), comes the logic of the function. The result is calculated.

Finally, the function uses a `return` statement to indicate that it has output. A `return` statement is not necessary, and if it is missing a function will return `None` by default. Furthermore, you can use more than one return statement, and they do not even have to be at the end of the function. For example a conditional block may contain a return statement inside of an `if` block and another in an `else` block.

To recap, the main parts of a function are:

- the `def` keyword

- a function name

- function parameters between parentheses

- a colon (`:`)

- indentation

- docstring

- logic

- return statement

19.1 Invoking functions

When you call or execute a function, that is known as *invoking* a function. In Python, it is easy to invoke functions by adding parentheses following the function name. This code invokes the newly defined function `add_2`:

```
>>> add_2(3)
5
```

To invoke a function, simple list its name, followed by a left parenthesis, the input parameters and a right parenthesis. Notice that the REPL implicitly prints the result—the integer 5. The result is what the `return` statement passes back.

19.2 Multiple parameters

Here is a function that takes two parameters and returns their sum:

```
>>> def add_two_nums(a, b):
...     return a + b
```

This function can add two integers:

```
>>> add_two_nums(4, 6)
10
```

It can also add floats:

```
>>> add_two_nums(4.0, 6.0)
10.0
```

It is also possible to add strings:

```
>>> add_two_nums('4', '6')
'46'
```

Note that the strings use + to perform string *concatenation* (joining two strings together).

If you try to add a string and a number, Python will complain though:

```
>>> add_two_nums('4', 6)
Traceback (most recent call last):
  File "<stdin>", line 1, in <module>
  File "<stdin>", line 2, in
  add_two_nums
TypeError: cannot concatenate 'str' and
'int' objects
```

This is an instance where Python wants you to be more specific about what operation is desired. If you want to add string types to numbers, it might be preferable to convert them to numbers first (using float or int). Likewise, it might be useful to convert from numbers to strings if concatenation is the desired operation. Python does not implicitly choose which operation. Rather it throws an error which should force the programmer to resolve the ambiguity.

19.3 Default parameters

One cool feature of Python functions is *default parameters*. Sometimes default parameters are referred to as *named parameters*. Like the name implies, default parameters allow you to specify the default values for function parameters. The default parameters are then optional, though you can override them if you need. The following function is similar to add_two_nums, but will default to adding 3 if the second number is not provided:

```
>>> def add_n(num, n=3):
...     """default to
...     adding 3"""
...     return num + n

>>> add_n(2)
5
>>> add_n(15, -5)
10
```

To create a default value for a parameter simply follow the parameter name by an equal sign (=) and the value.

> **Tip**
>
> Default parameters must be declared after non-default parameters. Otherwise Python will give you a SyntaxError:
>
> ```
> >>> def add_n(num=3, n):
> ...     return num + n
>   File "<stdin>", line 1
> SyntaxError: non-default argument follows
> default argument
> ```

> **Tip**
>
> Do not use mutable types (lists, dictionaries) for default parameters unless you know what you are doing. Because of the way Python works, the default parameters are created only once—when a function is defined.

Tip (cont.)

If you use a mutable default value, you will end up reusing the same instance of the default parameter during each function invocation:

```
>>> def to_list(value, default=[]):
...     default.append(value)
...     return default

>>> to_list(4)
[4]
>>> to_list('hello')
[4, 'hello']
```

The fact that default parameters are instantiated at the time the function is created is considered a wart by many people. This is because the behavior can be suprising. The commonly used work around is to have the parameter default to None, and create an instance of the default type within the body of the function if the default is None:

```
>>> def to_list2(value,
...               default=None):
...     if default is None:
...         default = []
...     default.append(value)
...     return default

>>> to_list2(4)
[4]
>>> to_list2('hello')
['hello']
```

If you want to be more succinct, the lines:

```
...     if default is None:
...         default = []
```

Can be written as a single line:

```
...     default = default or []
```

19.4   Naming conventions for functions

Function naming conventions are similar to variable naming conventions (and are also found in the PEP 8 document). Function names should:

- be lowercase

- have_an_underscore_between_words

- not start with numbers

- not override built-ins

- not be a keyword

Chapter 20

Indexing and Slicing

Two nice constructs that Python provides to pull data out of sequence-like types (lists, tuples, and even strings) are *indexing* and *slicing*. Indexing allows you to access single items out of a sequence, while slicing allows you to pull out a sub-sequence from a sequence.

20.1 Indexing

For example, if you have a list containing pets, you can pull out animals by index:

```
>>> my_pets = ["dog", "cat", "bird"]
>>> print my_pets[0]
dog
>>> print my_pets[-1]
bird
```

Tip

Indices start at 0. If you want to pull out the first item you reference it by 0, not 1. This is *zero-based indexing*.

> **Tip**
>
> You can also reference items using negative indices. -1 references the last item, -2 the second to last item, etc. This is especially useful for pulling off the last item.

20.2   Slicing sub lists

In addition to accepting an integer to pull out a single item, a *slice* may be used to pull out a sub-sequence. A slice may contain the start index, the end index (up to thes value but not including), and a *stride*, all separated by a colon.

Here is a slice to pull out the first two items of a list:

```
>>> my_pets = ["dog", "cat", "bird"]  # a list
>>> print my_pets[0:2]
['dog', 'cat']
```

Remember that Python uses the *half-open interval* convention. The list goes up to but does not include the end index. As mentioned previously, the range function also behaves similarly with its second parameter.

If you include the colon (:), the first index is optional. If the first index is missing, the slice defaults to the first item of the list (the zeroth item):

```
>>> print my_pets[:2]
['dog', 'cat']
```

You can also negative indices when slicing. It works for either the first or second index. An index of -1 would be the last item. If you slice up to the last item, you will get everything but that item (remember Python usually goes up to but not including the end range):

```
>>> my_pets[0:-1]
['dog', 'cat']
>>> my_pets[:-1]  # defaults to 0
['dog', 'cat']

>>> my_pets[0:-2]
['dog']
```

If you include the colon (:), the final index is optional. If the final index is missing, the slice defaults to the end of the list:

```
>>> my_pets[1:]
['cat', 'bird']
>>> my_pets[-2:]
['cat', 'bird']
```

If you include the colon (:), the first and second indices are optional. If both indices are missing, the slice returned will contain a copy of the list. This is actually a construct you see to quickly copy lists in Python.

```
>>> print my\_pets[:]
['dog', 'cat', 'bird']
```

20.3 Striding slices

Slices can also take a *stride* following the starting and ending indices. The default value for a stride when unspecified is 1, which means to take every item from a sequence between the indices. A stride of 2 would take every second item. A stride of 3 would take every third item:

```
>>> my_pets = ["dog", "cat", "bird"]
>>> dog_and_bird = my_pets[0:3:2]
>>> print dog_and_bird
['dog', 'bird']

>>> zero_three_six = [0, 1, 2, 3, 4, 5, 6][::3]
>>> print zero_three_six
[0, 3, 6]
```

> **Note**
>
> Again, the range function has a similar third parameter that specifies stride.

Strides can be negative. A stride of -1 means that you move backwards right to left. If you want to use a negative stride, you should make the start slice greater than the end slice. The exception for this is if you leave out the start and end indices a stride of -1 will reverse the sequence:

```
>>> my_pets[0:2:-1]
[]
>>> my_pets[2:0:-1]
['bird', 'cat']

>>> print [1, 2, 3, 4][::-1]
[4, 3, 2, 1]
```

Chapter 21

File Input and Output

One common use of programs is to read and write files. Python makes these operations easy. The built-in function open allows you to open a file for reading or writing.

21.1 Opening files

The built-in function open returns a file object. The file object has various methods to allow for reading and writing. This chapter discusses the most commonly used methods. To read the full documentation on a file object just pass it to the help function. It will list all the methods and describe what they do:

```
>>> a_file = open('/tmp/a.txt', 'w')
>>> help(a_file)
Help on file object:

class file(object)
 |  file(name[, mode[, buffering]]) -> file object
 |
 |  Open a file.  The mode can be 'r', 'w' or 'a'
...
```

21.2 Reading files

If you want to read a single line from an existing file, it is simple using the `readline` method:

```
>>> passwd_file = open('/etc/passwd')
>>> print passwd_file.readline()
root:x:0:0:root:/root:/bin/bash
```

Be careful, if you try to read a file that does not exist, Python will throw an error:

```
>>> fin = open('bad_file')
Traceback (most recent call last):
  File "<stdin>", line 1, in <module>
IOError: [Errno 2] No such file or
directory: 'bad_file'
```

Tip

The open function returns a *file object* instance. This object has methods to read and write data. You might be tempted to name a variable `file`. Try not to since `file` is a built-in function.

Common variable names for file objects that do not override built-ins are `fin` (file input), `fout` (file output), `fp` (file pointer, used for either input or output) or names such as `passwd_file`. Names like `fin` and `fout` are useful because they indicate whether the file is used for reading or writing respectively.

As illustrated above, the `readline` method will return one line of a file. You can call it repeatedly to retrieve every line, or use the `readlines` method to return a list containing all the lines.

To read all the contents of a file into one string use the `read` method:

```
>>> print open('/etc/passwd').read()
root:x:0:0:root:/root:/bin/bash
bin:x:1:1:bin:/bin:/bin/false
daemon:x:2:2:daemon:/sbin:/bin/false
adm:x:3:4:adm:/var/adm:/bin/false
```

21.3 Iteration with files

Iteration over sequences was discussed previously. In Python it is really easy to iterate over the lines in a file. If you are dealing with a text file, the readlines method will iterate over every line:

```
>>> fin = open('/etc/passwd')
>>> for line in fin.readlines():
...     print line
```

Because readlines returns a list—and lists support iterating over them—the above example should be straightforward. Python has a trick up its sleeve though. Python allows you to loop over the file instance itself to iterate over the lines of the file:

```
>>> fin = open('/etc/passwd')
>>> for line in fin:
...     print line
```

How does that work? Python has a dunder method, __iter__ that defines what the behavior is for looping over an instance. It just so happens that for a file this method is implemented to iterate over the lines in the file.

Tip

In addition to typing a few less characters for line iteration, the __iter__ method has an additional benefit. Rather than loading all the lines into memory at once, it reads the lines one at a time. If you happen to be examining a large log file, readlines will read the whole file into memory. If the file is large enough, this might fail. However, looping over lines in the file with __iter__ will not fail even for large text files since in only reads one line from a file at a time.

119

21.4 Writing files

To write to a file, you must first open the file in *write* mode. This is done by passing the 'w' string in as the second parameter to open:

```
>>> fout = open('/tmp/names.txt', 'w')
>>> fout.write('George')
```

The above method will overwrite the file /tmp/names.txt if it exists, otherwise it will create it.

Two methods used to place data in a file are write and writelines. write takes a string as a parameter and writes it to the file. writelines takes a sequence containing string data and writes it to the file.

Note

If you want to include newlines in your file you need to explicitly pass them to the file methods. On unix platforms, strings passed into write should end with \n. Likewise, each of the strings in the sequence that is passed into to writelines should end in \n. On Windows, the newline string is \r\n.

To program in a cross platform manner, the linesep string found in the os module defines the correct newline string for the platform.

Tip

If you are trying this out on the interpreter right now, you may notice that the /tmp/names.txt file is empty even though you told Python to write George in it. What is going on?

File output is *buffered* by Python. In order to optimize writes to the storage media, Python will only write data after a certain threshold has been passed. On Linux systems this is normally 4K bytes.

Tip (cont.)

To force writing the data, you can call the flush method, which *flushes* the pending data to the storage media.

A more heavy-handed mechanism, to ensure that data is written, is to call the close method. This informs Python that you are done writing to the file:

```
>>> fout2 = open('/tmp/names2.txt',
...              'w')
>>> fout2.write('John\n')
>>> fout2.close()
```

21.5 Closing files

As mentioned previously, calling close will write the file buffers out to the storage media. It is considered a good practice to always close files after you are done with them (whether for writing or reading). Operating systems have limits to how many files can be open at once.

In Python 2.5, the with statement was introduced. The with statement is used with *context managers* to enforce conditions before and after a block is executed. The open function now serves as a context manager to ensure that a file is closed when the block is left. Here is an example:

```
>>> with open('/tmp/names3.txt',
...           'w') as fout3:
...     fout3.write('Ringo\n')
```

This is the equivalent of:

```
>>> fout3 = open('/tmp/names3.txt',
...              'w')
>>> fout3.write('Ringo\n')
>>> fout3.close()
```

Notice that the with line ends with a colon. Indented content following a colon is a *block*. In the above example, the block consisted of writing Ringo to a file. Then the block finished. At this point the context manager kicks in. The file

context manager tells Python to automatically close the file
for you when the block is finished.

> **Tip**
>
> Use the with construct for reading and writing files.
> It is a good practice to close files, and if you use with
> you do not have to worry about it, since it automatically
> closes the files for you.

21.6 Designing around files

If your program becomes semi-complex, you will probably
be organizing your code into functions. One benefit to using
functions is that you can re-use those functions throughout
your code. Here is a tip for organizing functions dealing with
files.

Assume that you want to write code to insert the line
number before every line. At first thought it might seem that
you want the *API* (application programming interface) for
your functions to accept the filename of the file that you want
to modify:

```
>>> def add_numbers(filename):
...     results = []
...     with open(filename) as fin:
...         for num, line in \
... enumerate(fin):
...             results.append(
... '{0}-{1}'.format(num, line))
...     return results
```

This code will probably work okay. But what will happen
when the requirement comes to insert line numbers in front
of lines not coming from files? Or if you want to test the code,
now you need to have access to the file system. One way
around this is to write add_numbers similar to above, but have
it call another function, add_nums_to_seq that actually adds
the line numbers to a sequence:

```
>>> def add_numbers(filename):
...     with open(filename) as fin:
```

```
...            return add_nums_to_seq(fin)
>>> def add_nums_to_seq(seq):
...      results = []
...      for num, line in \
...          enumerate(seq):
...          results.append(
... '{0}-{1}'.format(num, line))
...      return results
```

Now you have a more general function, add_nums_to_seq that is easier to test and reuse, because instead of depending on a filename, it just depends on a sequence.

Hint

Actually there are other types that implement the file-like interface (read and write). Anytime you find yourself coding with a filename, ask yourself if you may want to apply the logic to other sequence like things. If so, use the previous example of nesting the functions to obtain code that is much easier to reuse.

Chapter 22

Classes

You have read about *objects*, such as strings, files, and integers. In Python almost everything is an object (keywords such as in are not objects). This chapter will delve deeper into what an object really is.

Object is a somewhat ambiguous term. When you hear about "Object Oriented Programming", it means grouping together data (state) and methods (functions to alter state). Many object oriented languages such as C++, Java, and Python use *classes* to define state and methods. Whereas classes are the definition of the state and methods, *instances* are occurrences of said classes.

For example, in Python, str is the name of the class used to store strings. The str class defines the methods of strings.

You can create an instance of the str class by using Python's literal string syntax:

```
# an instance of a String
>>> "I'm a string"
I'm a string
```

> **Note**
>
> The str class can also be used to create strings, but is normally used for casting. It is a bit of overkill to pass in a string literal into the str class.

You hear that Python comes with "batteries included"—it has libraries and classes predefined for your use. But you can also define your own classes, and then create instances of them.

22.1 Defining a class

Here is a simple class to represent a named animal:

```
>>> class Animal(object):
...     '''
...     An animal that has a name
...     '''
...     def __init__(self, name):
...         self.name = name
...
...     def talk(self):
...         '''
...         Make this animal speak
...         '''
...         print "Generic Animal Sound"
```

There are a few things to notice here. First, the keyword class indicates the definition of a class. This is followed by the name of the class—Animal. In Python 2.x, the class name is normally followed by a superclass, (object) in this case.

The last character on the line is the colon (:). Remember that a colon indicates that you are going to define a block. In this case the block will be the code describing the state and methods on the class. Note that everything below that first colon is indented.

> **Note**
>
> Class names are normally *camel cased*. Unlike functions where words are joined together with underscores, in camel casing, you capitalize the first letter of each word and then shove them together. Normally class names are nouns. In Python they cannot start with numbers. The following are examples of class names both good and bad:
>
> • Kitten # good

Note (cont.)

- jaguar # bad - starts with lowercase

- SnowLeopard # good - camel case

- White_Tiger # bad - has underscores

- 9Lives # bad - starts with a number

See PEP 8 for further insight into class naming.

Note that many of the built-in types do not follow this rule: str, int, float, etc.

Inside of the body of a class are *methods*. You have already seen many methods, such as format on a string. Methods are simply functions that are attached to a class. Instead of calling the method by itself, you need to call it on an instance of the class.

The first method defined is the __init__ (dunder init) method. This is a special *constructor* method that is called when you create an instance of the class. Inside a constructor you bind data to the instance.

Normally, most class methods have self as their first parameter. self is a reference to the instance of the class. In the __init__ method, the name is also passed in as a parameter and bound to the instance of the animal as name. This is in essence creating the "state" of the animal, and in this case the only state that it stores is the name.

Following __init__ you define talk, a method that just prints out Generic animal sound when it is called. Note that this is a method, it also has self as its first parameter. Whereas the __init__ method initializes the state of an instance, the other methods are normally responsible to mutate the instance or perform actions with it.

> **Note**
>
> Classes and their methods can have docstrings. These are useful while browsing code, and are accessible from the REPL by invoking `help` on the class name:
>
> ```
> >>> help(Animal)
> Help on class Animal in module
> __main__:
>
> class Animal(__builtin__.object)
>  |  An animal that has a name
>  |
>  |  Methods defined here:
>  |
>  |  __init__(self, name)
>  |
>  |  talk(self)
>  |      Make this animal speak
> ```

22.2   Creating an instance of a class

Now that you have defined a class, you can easily create instances of the class:

```
>>> animal = Animal("thing")
```

In the above Animal is the class to create, and animal is a variable holding the instance of the class. The animal variable now refences an instance of Animal. This instance has "state", which consists of a name, "thing". When the instance of the class is *instantiated* or created, the constructor (`__init__`) is called. Within the body of the constructor you can define the state of an instance by binding data to self.

22.3   Calling a method on a class

Now that you have an instance of a class, you can call methods on it. Methods are invoked by adding parentheses with any arguments inside of them. The talk method does not require arguments, Python takes care of passing self automatically:

```
>>> animal.talk()
Generic Animal Sound
```

22.4 Examining an instance

If you have an instance and would like to know what its attributes are, you have a few options. You can look up the documentation (if it exists). You can read the code where the class was defined. Or you can use dir to examine it for you:

```
>>> dir(animal)
['__class__', '__delattr__',
'__dict__', '__doc__', '__format__',
'__getattribute__', '__hash__',
'__init__', '__module__', '__new__',
'__reduce__', '__reduce_ex__',
'__repr__', '__setattr__',
'__sizeof__', '__str__',
'__subclasshook__', '__weakref__',
'name', 'talk']
```

Note that an instance of animal has the attributes for both the data bound to the instance (in the __init__ method), as well as any methods defined. You see the name attribute for the data and the talk attribute for the method.

129

Chapter 23

Subclassing a Class

Besides grouping state and action in a coherent place, classes also enable re-use. One way to re-use them is to *subclass* an existing class, or *superclass*. (Another common term for superclass is *parent class*). If you wanted to create a class representing a Cat, which is a more specialized version of an Animal, you can create a subclass. Subclasses allow you to inherit methods of parent classes, and override methods you want to tweak.

Here is the class Cat, which is a subclass of Animal:

```
>>> class Cat(Animal):
...     def talk(self):
...         print '%s says, "Meow!"' %\
...             self.name
```

When Animal was defined, the first line defining the class was class Animal(object). This tells Python to create a class Animal that is more specialized than object, the *base class*. Here the line defining the class, class Cat(Animal), indicates the definition of a new class, Cat that is more specific than the base class of Animal.

Because Cat defines talk, that method is *overridden*. The constructor, __init__, was not overriden, so Cat uses the same constructor as its superclass.

By overriding methods, you can further specialize a class. If you do not need to override, you can encourage code reuse, which is nice because it eliminates typing, but also can eliminate bugs.

Here is an example of instantiating a cat and calling a method on it:

```
>>> cat = Cat("Groucho")
>>> cat.talk() # invoke method
Groucho says, "Meow!"
```

23.1 Superclasses

The class definitions of Animal and Cat indicated that their superclasses are object and Cat respectively. If you are coming from a language like Java, this might be somewhat confusing. Why should Animal have a superclass, when it should be the baseclass?

In reality, using object as the superclass of Animal is not required in Python 2.x, but Python 2.2 introduced a change to allow subclassing of lists and dicts, which changed the underlying implementation for classes. This change introduced *new-style classes* which should derive from object. The original *classic class* is still available in Python 2.x, when a class is defined without a baseclass:

```
>>> class ClassicCat:
...     'classic class style'
...     def __init__(self, name):
...         self.name = name
```

But classic classes cannot derive from dict or list types. Nor can they have *properties* defined on them. Also the *method resolution order*, which parent classes to call for methods, is different for both types of classes.

Tip

Superclasses can be confusing because they have changed in Python 2 and again in Python 3.

In Python 3.x the (object) is not required. If you do not use it in Python 2.x you will create what is known as a "classic" class. In this case the old school style is

---

> **Tip (cont.)**
>
> bad, so use (object) in 2.x. But in 3.x you do not need to. Yes, Python 3.x cleaned up that wart, but it is now somewhat confusing.

23.2   Calling parent class methods

In the previous example Cat is the *subclass*, Animal is the *superclass* or *parent class*. Sometimes you want to override some of the parent class's definition, but also use some of its behavior. You need a way to call the implementation of the parent class from the subclass. The super function allows access to a parent class's implementation. Here is a new class, TomCat, that subclasses Cat. TomCat behaves similar to Cat but belches after speaking:

```
>>> class TomCat(Cat):
...     def talk(self):
...         # call parent method
...         super(TomCat, self).talk()
...         print "Burp!"

>>> rude_cat = TomCat("Fred")
>>> rude_cat.talk()
Fred says, "Meow!"
Burp!
```

> **Note**
>
> The semantics of super are interesting. You pass in the name of the class (TomCat) and the class instance (self), and super will return the superclass on which you can call the superclass' method. Also super only works on new-style classes.
>
> In Python 3 the semantics of super have been simplified and super().talk() would work on the example above.
>
> There are two cases where super really comes in handy. One is for resolving method resolution order

133

Note (cont.)

(*MRO*) in classes that have multiple parents. super will guarantee that this order is consistent. The other is when you change the base class, super is intelligent about determining who the new base is. This aids in code maintainability.

The old school way (before Python 2.2, when super was introduced) was just to invoke the method on the parent. It still works in a pinch on all Python versions:

```
>>> class TomCat(Cat):
...     def talk(self):
...         # call parent method
...         TomCat.talk(self)
...         print "Burp!"
```

Chapter 24

Exceptions

Often a computer is told to perform an action that it cannot do. Reading files that do not exist or dividing by zero are two examples. Python allows you to deal with such *exceptions* when they occur. When these cases occur, Python *throws an exception*, or *raises an exception*.

Normally when an exception occurs Python will halt and print out a *stack trace* explaining where the problem occurred. This is useful in that it tells you where your problem occurred:

```
>>> 3/0
Traceback (most recent call last):
  File "<stdin>", line 1, in <module>
ZeroDivisionError: integer division
or modulo by zero
```

The above states that in line 1 there was a divide by zero error. When you execute a program with an exception, the stack trace will indicate the file name and line number of where the problem occurred.

24.1 Look before you leap

Suppose you have a program that performs division. Depending on how it is coded, it may be possible that it tries to divide by zero at some point. There are two styles for dealing with exceptions that are commonly used with Python. The first is *look before you leap*. The idea is to check for exceptional cases before performing an action. In this case examine the denominator value and determine if it is zero or not. If it is not zero the program could perform the division, otherwise it could skip it.

This can be achieved in Python using `if` statements:

```
>>> numerator = 10
>>> divisor = 0
>>> if divisor != 0:
...     result = numerator / divisor
... else:
...     result = None
```

Note

Note that None is used to represent the undefined state. This is a common idiom throughout Pythondom. Be careful though, not to try and invoke methods on a variable that contains None.

24.2   Easier to ask for forgiveness

Another option for dealing with exceptions is known as *easier to ask for forgiveness than permission*. The idea here is to always perform the operation inside of a *try* block. If the operation fails the exception will be *caught* by the *exception* block.

The `try...except` construct provides a mechanism for Python to catch exceptional cases:

```
>>> numerator = 10
>>> divisor = 0
>>> try:
...     result = numerator / divisor
... except ZeroDivisionError as e:
...     result = None
```

Notice that the `try` construct creates a block following the `try` statement (because there is colon and indentation). Inside of the try block are the statements that might throw an exception. If the statements actually throw an exception Python looks for an except block that *catches* that exception. Here the except block states that it will catch any exception that is an instance (or sublass) of the `ZeroDivisionError` class. If an error in thrown in the `try` block, the `except` block is executed and `result` is set to `None`.

Tip

Try to limit the scope of the `try` block. Instead of including all of the code in a function inside a `try` block, put only the line that will possibly throw the error.

Tip

Which method is better? It depends. If you find yourself running into exceptions often it is possible that look before you leap might be favorable. Raising exceptions and catching them is a relatively expensive operation.

Here are some good rules of thumb for exception handling:

- Gracefully handle errors you know how to handle and can reasonably expect.

- Do not silence exceptions that you cannot handle or do not reasonably expect.

- Use a global exception handler to gracefully handle unexpected errors.

24.3 Multiple exceptional cases

If there are multiple exceptions that your code needs to be aware of, you can chain a list of except statements together:

```
>>> try:
...     some_function()
... except ZeroDivisionError, e:
...     # handle specific
... except Exception, e:
...     # handle others
```

In this case, when some_function throws an exception, the interpreter checks first if it is a ZeroDivisionError (or subclass of it). If that is not the case, it check it the exception is a sublass of Exception. Once an except block is entered, Python no longer check the subsequent blocks.

If an exception is not handled by the chain, it will be re-raised at the end of the try block.

24.4 finally **clause**

Another clause that can be used in error handling is the finally clause. This is used to place code that will always execute, whether an exception happens or not. If the try block succeeds, then the finally block will be executed.

If an exception is raised, finally always executes. If the exception is handled, the finally block will execute after the handling. If the exception is not handled, the finally block will execute and then the exception will be re-raised:

```
>>> try:
...     some_function()
... except Exception, e:
...     # handle errors
... finally:
...     # cleanup
```

Usually the purpose of finally clause is to handle external resources, such as files, network connections, or databases. These should be freed regardless of whether an operation was successful or not.

24.5 else **clause**

The optional else clause in a try statement is executed when no exception is raised. It must follow any except statements, and executes before the finally block:

```
>>> try:
...     print 'hi'
... except Exception, e:
...     print 'Error'
... else:
```

```
...      print 'Success'
... finally:
...      print 'at last'
hi
Success
at last
```

24.6 Raising exceptions

Python also allows you to raise exceptions (or throw them). Exceptions are subclasses of the BaseException class, and are easily raised using the raise statement:

```
>>> raise BaseException('Program failed')
```

Normally you will not raise the generic BaseException class, but will raise subclasses that are predefined, or define your own.

24.7 Defining your own exceptions

Python has many built-in exceptions defined in the exceptions module. If your error corresponds well with the existing exceptions, you can re-use them. Using help you can list the exceptions, and see their class hierarchy:

```
>>> import exceptions
>>> help(exceptions)
Help on built-in module exceptions:
 ...
CLASSES
    __builtin__.object
        BaseException
            Exception
                StandardError
                    ArithmeticError
                        FloatingPointError
                        OverflowError
                        ZeroDivisionError
                    AssertionError
                    AttributeError
                    BufferError
                    EOFError
                    EnvironmentError
                        IOError
```

139

```
                    OSError
            ImportError
            LookupError
                IndexError
                KeyError
            MemoryError
            NameError
                UnboundLocalError
            ReferenceError
            RuntimeError
                NotImplementedError
            SyntaxError
                IndentationError
                    TabError
            SystemError
            TypeError
            ValueError
                UnicodeError
                    UnicodeDecodeError
                    UnicodeEncodeError
                    UnicodeTranslateError
        StopIteration
        Warning
            BytesWarning
            DeprecationWarning
            FutureWarning
            ImportWarning
            PendingDeprecationWarning
            RuntimeWarning
            SyntaxWarning
            UnicodeWarning
            UserWarning
    GeneratorExit
    KeyboardInterrupt
    SystemExit
```

When defining your own exception, you should subclass
from Exception or below.

Here is an exception for defining that a program is missing
information:

```
>>> class DataError(Exception):
...     def __init__(self, missing):
...         self.missing = missing
```

Using it in code is easy:

```
>>> if 'important_data' not in config:
...     raise DataError('important_data')
```

Chapter 25

Importing libraries

The previous chapters have covered the basic constructs for Python. In this chapter you'll learn about importing code. Many languages have the concept of *libraries* or reusable chunks of code. Python comes with "batteries included", which really means that the standard libraries that come included with Python should allow you to do a lot without having to look elsewhere.

To use libraries you have to load the code into your *namespace*. The namespace holds the functions, classes, and variables (ie "names") your module has access to. For example the built-in math library has a sin function that calculates the sine of an angle expressed in radians:

```
>>> from math import sin
>>> sin(0)
0.0
```

The above code loads the sin function from the math module into your namespace. If you do this from the REPL as illustrated above, you have access to the sin function from the REPL. If you include that code in a file, code in that file should now have access to the sin function.

25.1 Multiple ways to import

In the previous example you only imported a single function from a library. It is also possible to load the library into your namespace and reference all its classes, functions, and variables:

```
>>> import math
>>> math.tan(0)
0.0
```

In the above we imported the math library and invoked its tan function.

Tip

When would you import a function using from or import a library using import? If you are using a couple of attributes of a library perhaps you might want to use a from style import. It is possible to specify multiple comma-delimted attributes in the from construct:

```
>>> from math import sin, cos, tan
>>> cos(0)
1.0
```

If you need access to most of the library, it is less typing to just import the library. It also serves as a hint to you as a programmer, where the function (or class or variable) is defined.

Note

Prior to Python 2.4 an import line could not span multiple lines unless backslashes were used to escape line endings:

```
>>> from math import sin,
...     cos
Traceback (most recent call last):
  File "<stdin>", line 1, in <module>
SyntaxError: trailing comma not allowed
without surrounding parentheses
```

> **Note (cont.)**
>
> But this works:
>
> ```
> >>> from math import sin,\
> ...    cos
> ```
>
> With PEP 328, Python 2.4 included the ability to specify multiple imports with parentheses:
>
> ```
> >>> from math import (sin,
> ...    cos)
> ```

25.2 Conflicting import names

If you were working on a program that performs trigonometric operations, you might already have a function named sin. What if you now want to use the sin function from the math library? One option is to just import math, then math.sin would reference the library and sin would reference your function. Another option is that Python allows you to redefine the name of what you what to import using the as keyword:

```
>>> from math import sin as other_sin
>>> other_sin(0)
0.0
```

Now other_sin is a reference to the sin found in math and you may continue using your sin without having to refactor your code.

The as keyword construct also works on import statements. If you had a variable (or a function) that conflicted with the math name in your namespace, the following would be one way to get around it:

```
>>> import math as other_math
>>> other_math.sin(0)
0.0
```

> **Tip**
>
> The as keyword can also be used to eliminate typing. If your favorite library has overly long and verbose names you can easily shorten them in your code. Users of the Numpy[¶] library have adopted the standard of reducing keystrokes by using a two letter acronym:
>
> ```
> >>> import numpy as np
> ```
>
> The Pandas[‖] library has adopted a similar standard:
>
> ```
> >>> import pandas as pd
> ```

25.3 Star imports

Python also allows you to clobber your namespace with what are known as star imports:

```
>>> from math import *
>>> asin(0)
0.0
```

Notice that the above calls the arc sine, which has not yet been defined. The line where `asin` is invoked is the first reference to `asin` in the code. What happened? When you say `from library import *`, it tells Python to throw everything from the library (class definitions, functions, and variables) into the local namespace. While this might appear handy at first glance, it is quite dangerous.

Star imports make debugging harder, because it is not explicit where code comes from. Even worse are star imports from multiple libraries. Subsequent library imports might override something defined in an earlier library. As such star imports are discouraged and frowned upon by many Python programmers.

[¶] numpy.scipy.org

[‖] pandas.pydata.org

> **Tip**
>
> Do not use star imports!

> **Note**
>
> The possible exceptions to this rule are when you are writing your own testing code, or messing around in the REPL. Library authors do this as a shortcut to importing everything from the library that they want to test. But just because you see it in testing code, do not be tempted to use it in other places.

25.4 Nested libraries

Some Python packages have a nested namespace. For example the xml library that comes with Python has support for minidom and etree. Both libraries live under the xml parent package:

```
>>> from xml.dom.minidom import \
... parseString
>>> dom = parseString(
...     '<xml><foo/></xml>')

>>> from xml.etree.ElementTree import \
...     XML
>>> elem = XML('<xml><foo/></xml>')
```

Notice that the from construct allows importing only the functions and classes needed. Using the import construct would require more typing (but also allow access to everything from the package):

```
>>> import xml.dom.minidom
>>> dom = xml.dom.minidom.parseString(
...     '<xml><foo/></xml>')

>>> import xml.etree.ElementTree
>>> elem = xml.etree.ElementTree.XML(
...     '<xml><foo/></xml>')
```

25.5   Import organization

According to PEP 8, place import statements at the top of file following the module docstring. There should be one import per line and imports should be grouped by:

- Standard library imports

- 3rd party imports

- Local package imports

An example module might have the following at the start:

```
#!/usr/bin/env python
"""
This module converts records into json
and shoves them into a database
"""
import json           # standard libs
import sys

import psycopg2        # 3rd party lib

import recordconverter  # local library
...
```

Tip

It is useful to organize the grouped imports alphabetically.

Tip

It can be useful to postpone some imports to:

- Avoid circular imports. If you are not able (or willing) to refactor to remove the circular import, it is possible to place the import statement within the function or method containing the code that invokes it.

Tip (cont.)

- Avoid importing modules that are not available on some systems.

- Avoid importing large modules that you may not use.

Chapter 26

Libraries: Packages and Modules

The previous chapter discussed how to import libraries. This chapter will describe what constitutes a library. There are two requirements for importing a library:

1. The library must be a *module* or a *package*

2. The library must exist in PYTHONPATH environment variable or sys.path Python variable.

26.1 Modules

Modules are just Python files that end in .py, and have a name that is importable. PEP 8 states that module filenames should be short and in lowercase. Underscores may be used for readability.

26.2 Packages

A *package* in Python is a directory that contains a file named __init__.py. The file named __init__.py can have any implementation it pleases or it can be empty. In addition the directory may contain an arbitrary number of modules and subpackages.

Here is an example from a portion of the directory layout of the popular sqlalchemy project (an Object Relational Mapper for databases):

```
sqlalchemy/
  __init__.py
  engine/
    __init__.py
    base.py
  schema.py
```

PEP 8 states that package names filenames should be short and lowercase. Underscores should not be used.

26.3 Importing packages

To import a package, simply import the package name (the directory name):

```
>>> import sqlalchemy
```

This will import the sqlalchemy/__init__.py file into the current namespace.

To import schema.py and use the Column, and ForeignKey classes, either of these would work:

```
>>> import sqlalchemy.schema
>>> col = sqlalchemy.schema.Column()
>>> fk = sqlalchemy.schema.\
...     ForeignKey()
```

   or:

```
>>> from sqlalchemy import schema
>>> col = schema.Column()
>>> fk = schema.ForeignKey()
```

Alternatively, if you only needed access to the Column class you can import just that class in the following two ways:

```
>>> import sqlalchemy.schema.Column
>>> col = sqlalchemy.schema.Column()
```

   or:

```
>>> from sqlalchemy.schema import \
...     Column
```

```
>>> col = Column()
```

26.4 PYTHONPATH

PYTHONPATH is simply an environment variable listing non-standard directories that Python looks for modules or packages in. It is usually empty by default. It is not necessary to change this unless you are developing code and want to use libraries that have not been installed.

If you had some code in /home/test/a/plot.py, but were working out of /home/test/b/, using PYTHONPATH allows access to that code. Otherwise, if plot.py was not *installed* using system or Python tools, trying to import it would raise an ImportError:

```
>>> import plot
Traceback (most recent call last):
  File "<stdin>", line 1, in <module>
ImportError: No module named plot
```

If you start Python by setting the PYTHONPATH, it indicates to Python where to look for libraries:

```
$ PYTHONPATH=/home/test/a python
Python 2.7.2 (default, Oct 27 2011, 21:39:38)
>>> import plot
>>> plot.histogram()
...
```

> **Tip**
>
> Python packages can be installed via package managers, Windows executables or Python specific tools such as Pip or easy_install.

26.5 sys.path

sys.path is accessible after importing the sys module that comes with Python. It lists all the directories that are scanned for Python modules and packages. If you inspect this variable

you will see all the locations that are scanned. It might look
something like this:

```
>>> import sys
>>> print sys.path
['', '/usr/lib/python2.6',
'/usr/lib64/python2.6',
'/usr/lib/python2.6/plat-linux2',
'/usr/lib/python2.6/lib-tk',
'/usr/lib64/python2.6/lib-tk',
'/usr/local/lib/python2.6/site-packages',
'/usr/lib/python2.6/site-packages',
'/usr/lib/python2.6/site-packages/Numeric',
'/usr/lib/python2.6/site-packages/PIL',
'/usr/lib/python2.6/site-packages/gst-0.10',
'/usr/lib/python2.6/site-packages/gtk-2.0']
```

Tip

If you find yourself encountering errors like this:

```
ImportError: No module named foo
```

Use sys.path to see if it has the directory holding
foo.py (if it is a module) or the parent of the foo/ directory (in the case of a package):

```
>>> import plot
Traceback (most recent call last):
  File "<stdin>", line 1, in <module>
ImportError: No module named plot
>>> sys.path.append('/home/test/a')
>>> import plot
>>> plot.histogram()
...
```

Alternatively you can set PYTHONPATH to point to that
directory from the command used to invoke Python.

Chapter 27

A complete example

This chapter covers how to layout code within a script. It includes the source for a simplified implementation of the Unix command cat. This will illustrate what is typically found within a file of code.

27.1 cat.py

Here is the contents of the Python implementation of cat. It only includes an option for adding line numbers (--number), but none of the other cat options:

```
#!/usr/bin/env python

"""A simple implementation the the unix ''cat''
command. It only implements the ''--number''
option. It is useful for illustrating file
layout and best practices in Python.

This is a triple quoted docstring for the whole
module (this file). If you import this module
somewhere else and run ''help(cat)'', you will
see this.

This docstring also contains a ''doctest'' which
serves as an example of programmatically using
the code. It also functions as a doctest. The
''doctest'' module can execute this docstring
and validate it by checking any output.
```

```
>>> import StringIO
>>> fin = StringIO.StringIO(\
...     'hello\nworld\n')
>>> fout = StringIO.StringIO()
>>> cat = Catter([fin],
...     show_numbers=True)
>>> cat.run(fout)
>>> print fout.getvalue()
     0  hello
     1  world
<BLANKLINE>
"""

import argparse
import logging
import sys

__version__ = '0.0.1'


logging.basicConfig(
    level=logging.DEBUG)


class Catter(object):
    """
    A class to concatenate files to
    standard out

    This is a class docstring,
    ``help(cat.Catter)`` would show
    this.
    """

    def __init__(self, files,
                 show_numbers=False):
        self.files = files
        self.show_numbers = show_numbers

    def run(self, fout):
        # use 6 spaces for numbers and right align
        fmt = '{0:>6}  {1}'
        count = 0
        for fin in self.files:
            logging.debug('catting {0}'.format(fin))
            for line in fin.readlines():
                if self.show_numbers:
                    fout.write(fmt.format(
                        count, line))
                    count += 1
```

```
                else:
                    fout.write(line)


def main(args):
    """
    Logic to run a cat with arguments
    """
    parser = argparse.ArgumentParser(
        description='Concatenate FILE(s), or '
        'standard input, to standard output')
    parser.add_argument('--version',
        action='version', version=__version__)
    parser.add_argument('-n', '--number',
        action='store_true',
        help='number all output lines')
    parser.add_argument('files', nargs='*',
        type=argparse.FileType('r'),
        default=[sys.stdin], metavar='FILE')
    parser.add_argument('--run-tests',
        action='store_true',
        help='run module tests')
    args = parser.parse_args(args)

    if args.run_tests:
        import doctest
        doctest.testmod()
    else:
        cat = Catter(args.files, args.number)
        cat.run(sys.stdout)
        logging.debug('done catting')

if __name__ == '__main__':
    main(sys.argv[1:])
```

27.2   Common layout

Here are the common components found in a Python module
in the order they are found:

- #!/usr/bin/env python (shebang) used if module also
  serves as a script.

- module docstring

- imports

- metadata/globals

- logging

- implementation

- testing

- if __name__ == '__main__': (used if module also serves as a script.)

- argparse

> **Note**
>
> The above list is a recommendation. Most of those items can be in an arbitrary order. And not every file will have all these items. For instance not every file needs to be runnable as a shell script.
>
> You are free to organize files how you please, but you do so at your own peril. Users of your code will likely complain (or submit patches). You will also appreciate code that follows the recommendation, since it will be quickly discoverable.

27.3 Shebang

The first line on a file that also used as a script is usually the *shebang* line (#!/usr/bin/env python). On Unix operating systems, this line is parsed to determine how to execute the script. Thus, this line is only included in files that are meant to be runnable as scripts.

> **Note**
> The Windows platform ignores the shebang line.

Note

Rather than hardcoding a specific path to Python, /usr/bin/env selects the first python executable found on the user's PATH. Tools such as virtualenv will modify your PATH to use a custom python executable.

Tip

If the directory containing the file is present in the user's PATH environment variable, and the file is executable, then the file name alone is sufficient for execution from a shell.

27.4 Docstring

A module may have a docstring as the first piece of code. Since a docstring serves as an overview of the module, it should contain a basic summary of the code. Also it may contain examples of using the module.

Tip

Python contains a library, doctest that can verify examples from an interactive interpreter. Using docstrings that contain REPL code snippets can serve both as documentation and simple sanity tests for your library.

cat.py includes doctest code at the end of its docstring. When cat.py runs with --run-tests, the doctest library will check any docstrings and validate the code found in them. Normally a non-developer end user would not see options for running tests in a script. In this case it is included as an example of using doctest.

27.5   Imports

Imports are usually included at the top of Python modules. The import lines are normally grouped by location of library. First come any libraries found in the Python standard library. Next come third party libraries. Finally listed are libraries that are local to the current code. Such organization allows end users of your code to quickly see imports, requirements, and where code is coming from.

27.6   Metadata and globals

If you have legitimate module level global variables define them after the imports. This makes it easy to scan a module quickly and determine what the globals are.

Global variables are defined at the module level and are accessible throughout that module and any module that imports it. Because Python allows any variable to be modified they are potentially dangerous. In addition, it is easier to understand code when variables are defined and modified only within the function scope. Then you can be sure of what data you have and who is changing it. If you have multiple places where a global variable is being modified (especially if it is from different modules) you are setting yourself up for a long debugging session.

One legitimate use for globals is to emulate *constants* found in other programming languages. A constant variable is a variable whose value does not change. PEP 8 states that globals should have names that are the same as variables except they should be capitalized. For example if you wanted to use the golden ratio you could define it like this:

```
>>> GOLDEN_RATIO = 1.618
```

> **Note**
>
> Though the Python language does not have support for constant data types, globals are often used to indicate that a variable should be constant.

> **Note**
>
> By defining constants as globals, and using well thought-out variable names, you can avoid a problem found in programming—"magic numbers". A magic number is a numbers sitting in code or formulas that is not stored in a variable. That in itself it bad enough, especially when someone else starts reading your code.
>
> Another problem with magic numbers is that the same value tends to propagate through the code over time. The solution to both these problems (context and repetition) is to put the value in a named variable. Having them in a variable gives context and naming around the number. It also allows you to easily change the value in one place.

In addition to global variables, there are also *metadata* variables found at that level. Metadata variables hold information about the module, such as author and version. Normally metadata variables are specified using "dunder" variables such as __author__.

For example, PEP 396 recommends that module version be specified in a string, __version__, at the global module level.

> **Note**
>
> It is a good idea to define a version for your library if you intend on releasing it to the wild. PEP 386 suggests best practices for how to declare version strings.

Other common metadata variables include author, license, date, and contact. If these were specified in code they might look like this:

```
__author__ = 'Matt Harrison'
__date__ = 'Jan 1, 2010'
__contact__ = 'matt_harrison <at> someplace.com'
__version__ = '0.1.1'
```

27.7 Logging

One more variable that is commonly declared at the global level is the logger for a module. The Python standard library includes the `logging` library that allows you to report different levels of information in well defined formats.

Multiple classes or functions in the same module will likely need to log information. It is common to just do initialization once at the global level and then reuse the logger handle that you get back throughout the module.

27.8 Other globals

You should not use global variables when local variable will suffice. The common globals found in Python code are metadata, constants, and logging.

It is not uncommon to see globals scattered about in sample code. Do not fall to the temptation to just copy this code. Place it into a function or a class. This will pay dividends in the future during debugging.

27.9 Implementation

Following any global and logging setup comes the actual meat of the code—the implementation. This is accomplished by defining functions and classes. The `Catter` class would be considered the core logic of the module.

27.10 Testing

Normally bonafide test code is separated from the implementation code. Python allows a small exception to this. Python docstrings can be defined at module, function, class, and method levels. Within docstrings, you can place Python REPL snippets illustrating how to use the function, class or module. These snippets, if well crafted and thought-out, can be effective in documenting common usage of the module. In addition, Python includes a library, `doctest`, that allows testing and validation of Python REPL snippets.

160

Another nice feature of doctest is validation of documentation. If your snippets once worked, but now they fail, either your code has changed or your snippets are wrong. You can easily find this out before end users start complaining to you.

Tip

doctest code can be in a stand-alone text file. To execute arbitrary files using doctest, use the testfile function:

```
>>> import doctest
>>> doctest.testfile('module_docs.txt')
```

Note

In addition to doctest, the Python standard library includes the unittest module that implements the common xUnit style methodology—setup, assert, and teardown. There are pro's and con's to both doctest and unittest styles of testing. doctest tends to be more difficult to debug, while unittest contains boilerplate code that is regarded as too Java-esque. It is possible to combine both to achieve well documented and well tested code.

27.11 if __name__ == '__main__':

At the bottom of most Python files meant to be run as scripts, you will find this somewhat curious if statement:

```
if __name__ == '__main__':
    sys.exit(main(sys.argv[1:]) or 0)
```

To understand the statement, you should understand the __name__ variable.

27.12   __name__

Python defines the module level variable __name__ for any
module you *import*, or any file you execute. Normally __name__'s
value is the name of the module:

```
>>> import sys
>>> sys.__name__
'sys'
>>> import xml.sax
>>> xml.sax.__name__
'xml.sax'
```

There is an exception to this rule. When a module is *executed* (ie python some_module.py), then the value of __name__
is the string "__main__".

In effect, the value of __name__ indicates whether a file is
being loaded as a library, or run as a script.

Note

It is easy to illustrate __name__.   Create a file,
some_module.py, with the following contents:

```
print "The __name__ is: {0}".format(__name__)
```

Now run a REPL and *import* this module:

```
>>> import some_module
The __name__ is: some_module
```

Now *execute* the module:

```
$ python some_module.py
 The __name__ is: __main__
```

It is a common idiom throughout Pythondom to place a
check at the bottom of a module that could also serve as a
script, to determine whether the file is being executed:

```
if __name__ == '__main__':
    sys.exit(main(sys.argv[1:]) or 0)
```

This simple statement will run the main function when
the file is executed. Conversely, if the file is used a module,

main will not be run automatically. It calls `sys.exit` with the return value of main (or 0 if main does not return an exit code) to behave as a good citizen in the Unix world.

> **Tip**
>
> Some people place the execution logic inside of `main` function directly under the `if __name__ == '__main__':` test. Reasons to actually put the logic in a function include:
>
> - The `main` function can be called by others
>
> - The `main` function can be tested easily with different arguments
>
> - Reduce the amount of code executing at the global level

By laying out your code as described in this chapter, you will be following best practices for Python code. This layout will also aid others needing to read your code.

Chapter 28

Onto Bigger and Better

At this point you should have a pretty good understanding of how Python programs work. You should feel comfortable using the Python REPL and exploring classes using `dir` and `help`.

What comes next? That is up to you. You should now have the prerequisites to use Python to create websites, GUI programs or numerical applications.

One huge benefit of Python is the various communities associated with the different areas of programming. There are local user groups, newsgroups, mailing lists and social networks for various aspects of Python. Most of these groups are welcoming to new programmers and willing to share their knowledge. Do not be afraid to try something new, Python makes it easy and most likely there are others who have similar interests.

Appendix A: Testing in Python

This section will discuss testing strategies using `unittest` and `doctest` in Python. It will assume you want to test latest internet sensation–an integer generation site called *Integr*! Imagine a web-based service that could convert a string like "2,5,8" to an actual list of the numbers 2, 5 and 8. Integers are quite useful for activities such as counting and if you hurry you can beat the market. Heavy thick clients have used Integr technology in the "Select Pages" box of printer dialogs for ages. Yet no one has had the foresight to bring this functionality to the internet. The critical feature you need to start out is the ability to demarcate individual integers by commas!

This chapter will consider implementing the basic logic of the integer web-service using tests.

The Stigma of Testing

Is testing a four letter word? No, it is actually seven letters, but many developers prefer to have another department test their code, as if testing is below them. Other developers figure that the users of the code will test it, so why expend the effort? Other shops hand-off the code after development is deemed "finished" and co-workers will tinker with it and try to break it.

The problem with finding bugs later in the development cycle is the cost of repairing them goes up. Now, a bug needs to be filed, a testing manager needs to review those bugs, the development manager needs to approve which bugs get fixed, and the developer needs to switch focus to come back and fix code they wrote ages ago.

The simplest way to address these costs is to find the bugs as early as you can. Writing the tests first is a strategy to deal with this. Rather than just providing the basics to fill the spec, the tests can become the specs and you will code to them.

Detour to `unittest`

Out of the box Python provides a library, unittest, which is a library that implements the *x-unit* pattern. If you are familiar with Java, junit is an implementation of the this same paradigm. The basic idea is to start from a well known state, call the code you want to test, and assert that something has happened. If the assertion fails, the code is broken and needs to fixed. Otherwise the assertion passes and all is well. Groups of tests can be collected into "suites" and the execution of these suites can be easily automated.

Here is some code for testing the initial spec:

```python
import unittest
import integr

class TestIntegr(unittest.TestCase):
    def setup(self):
        # setup is called *before* each test is run
        # if I need to adjust to a well known state
        # before starting
        pass

    def teardown(self):
        # teardown is called *after* the each test
        # is run
        pass

    def test_basic(self):
        # any method beginning with "test" is a test
        results = integr.parse('1,3,4')
        self.assertEquals(results, [1,3,4])

if __name__ == '__main__':
    unittest.main()
```

unittest **details**

Unit tests are meant to test a single *unit* of code. A unit test
tests a single method or function (if your code is broken down
into functions that perform a single concrete action). The
goal of unit testing is to insure that the individual chunks
of code are acting as they should. There are other types of
testing as well, such as performance and integration testing,
whose goals are different that those of unit tests. Rather than
verifying logic of small blocks, these tests would measure
performance and ensure that disparate systems work in har-
mony.

Creating a unit test in Python is easy. At the most basic
level you subclass the unittest.TestCase class and implement methods that start with test.

Note

Any method that starts with test, will be treated as
a unit test. Even though PEP 8 encourages one to use
underscores (_) between words in function and method
names, unittest supports camel casing as well. In fact
the implementation of unittest itself disregards the
PEP 8 naming recommendations in favor of a following
a more Java-like style.

Notice the lines found at the bottom of the previous code:

```
>>> if __name__ == '__main__':
...     unittest.main()
```

When executed, unittest.main looks for all subclasses of
unittest.TestCase and then for every method starting with
"test", unittest will then call:

- the setup method

- the method starting with "test"

- the teardown method

The setup method is used to create a well known starting place for your tests. You know the old saying "Garbage in, garbage out"? It applies here, you want your tests to run *deterministically*, and if they depend on the state of something that may change, that makes it hard to run consistently. It is preferable to start and end each test in a known state. The setup method is where this is done. It is common for data driven applications to create or delete entries in databases here to ensure the asserted logic is run correctly.

Likewise, teardown is called after every test method. You can use it to clean up the state. If there are any changes to the environment that are set up for testing, such as files are directories, you can clean them out in teardown.

Having said that, for many low level unit tests, you will not need any setup or teardown methods. You will just be implementing the test methods.

What happens inside a test method is simple. You call out to a unit of code and then *assert* that something happened. It could be that a result was returned, an error was thrown, or nothing happened. You just need to have a way to *assert* this. Luckily the baseclass, unittest.TestCase, provides many methods for you to do this. The most basic is assert_(expression, [message]) (note the "_" because assert is a Python keyword). If the expression evaluates to false during execution, unittest will report that the assert failed at the corresponding location. If message is provided, it will be used in the reporting of the failed assertion.

Assertion Methods

Method signature	Explanation
assert_(expression, [message])	Complains if expression is False
assertEqual(this, that, [message])	Complains if this != that
assertNotEqual(this, that, [message])	Complains if this == that
assertRaises(exception, callable, *args, **kw)	Complains if callable(*args, **kw) does not raise exception (Made context manager in 2.7)
fail([message])	Complains immediately

There are other methods, but these are what you will be using 99% of the time for assertion. Python 2.7 added many new methods for assertions, cleanup during exceptional cases in setUp and tearDown, decorators for skipping tests on certain platforms and test discovery.

Running the test code

Now you have a basic test in testintegr.py. Let's run it:

```
$ python testintegr.py
Traceback (most recent call last):
  File "testintegr.py", line 1, in <module>
    import integr
ImportError: No module named integr
```

Of course there is an error at this point because integr has yet to be implemented. Now that you have the test in place, you can use it as a spec to code against.

Start with commas

This chapter leaves it up to you to implement the actual logic. If you feel so inclined, create a file integr.py in the same

171

directory as the `testintegr.py` file. Here is the starting code for it:

```
def parse(input):
    # fill this in
```

After writing your code, re-run your test. Does it work? If so, you are off on the right track to creating the next internet sensation.

Being controlled by testing

Following this manner of development, you can continue to work on the `integr` module. If you add the desired functionality to the test case first, you are following a practice known as *Test Driven Development* (TDD). The main idea of TDD is to write tests that initially fail for logic that you know you will need, and then go back and implement the logic to make the tests pass.

Just to beat in the point, here is another example. Because users cannot be expected to share your mental model of how an application functions, they could (and often will just for fun) provide input that you aren't expecting. Normal users might insert something that seems intuitive to them, like 2, 3 (note the space following the comma). Others might attempt more nefarious input such as "2,3<script> alert('foo'); </script>". The goal should be to gracefully handle most if not all input.

Handling Whitespace

To implement whitespace handling utilizing TDD, first add another test method to `testinteger.py`:

```
def test_spaces(self):
    results = integr.parse('1, 3, 4 ')
    self.assertEquals(results, [1,3,4])
```

Now when you run your test suite, the original `test_basic` method should pass and `test_spaces` should fail. Having a failing test case gives you a clear direction of what you need to develop. This is a compelling feature of TDD. Not only do you have tests, but if you develop the tests of the required functionality first, you will spend your time working on the desired functionality. Writing the test first also allows you to think about the API of your code.

This is not to say that the TDD methodology is a panacea. It certainly requires a small amount of determination (or gentle persuasion by a manager) to implement, but this upfront effort has both short and longterm benefits.

Exception Handling

Suppose input is unparseable and the spec says that `integr` should raise a `BadInput` exception. `unittest` provides a few ways for that:

```
def test_bad(self):
    self.assertRaises(BadInput, integr.parse, 'abcd')
```

Passing is a *callable* to `assertRaises` makes this a little less readable. Another options is:

```
def test_bad2(self):
    try:
        integr.parse('abcd')
        self.fail('Parsed bad input')
    except BadInput:
        pass
```

In Python 2.7+, `assertRaises` is a *context manager*, so it is written with a little less boilerplate:

```
def test_bad3(self):
    with self.assertRaises(BadInput):
        integr.parse('abcd')
```

> **Note**
>
> The new `unittest` features found in Python 2.7+ are available as a 3rd party package for Python 2.4+ users. This package is called `unittest2` and available at pypi.

TDD vs Code first

What comes to your mind when you write your tests before your code? Do you feel burdened by writing more tests? Or is it liberating to know be defining your API and then actually using it? Is it comforting knowing that in the future when you refactor the implementation that you will have a suite of tests to ensure that everything still works? TDD adherents claim that having to write the tests actually allows them to implement faster by focusing only on needed features and completing those features (even though they are writing more code, since they are writing the both code and the tests for the code), while ignoring premature optimization or featuritis.

The unittest module included in Python provides a simple interface for generating tests. The x-unit style is familiar to most who have written tests in other languages. It can be used in a TDD like manner but also supports the more traditional approach of writing tests when needed.

Turning testing on its head

Imagine reading the following post to the Python newsgroup:

- Examples are priceless.

- Examples that don't work are worse than worthless.

- Examples that work eventually turn into examples that don't.

- Docstrings too often don't get written.

- Docstrings that do get written rarely contain those priceless examples.

- The rare written docstrings that do contain priceless examples eventually turn into rare docstrings with examples that don't work. I think this one may follow from the above ...

- Module unit tests too often don't get written.

- The best Python testing gets done in interactive mode, esp. trying endcases that almost never make it into a test suite because they're so tedious to code up.

- The endcases that were tested interactively (but never coded up) also fail to work after time.

This sounds like someone had some gripes with the lack of both documentation and testing in software projects. The above points were actually taken from a snippet of a post that Tim Peters wrote to the *comp.lang.python* newsgroup in 1999 to enumerate the reasons for creating a new module called `doctest`.

Mr. Peters makes some good points. It is true, examples are priceless. How many people code simply by copying and pasting examples? How much software has good documentation? Or any documentation? Most developers are not concerned with documentation, so documentation is commonly non-existant. And many developers do not like testing. This oftentimes puts one in a pickle when picking up a new library.

Since the time of Mr. Peters' post, newer programming methodologies with more emphasis on testing have come out, so the situation might be better. Nonetheless, the ideas are compelling—what if you could somehow provide examples and documentation that also could serve as testcases?

Test my docstrings

Docstrings can be located on a module, class, method or function. While they can serve as examples of the API, they can also serve as tests. Creating a *doctest* is quite simple. Any docstring that has >>> followed by Python code can serve as a doctest. If you are developing with a REPL alongside, you can simply copy and paste the code out of it. Here is a trivial example of creating docstrings and executing them with the doctest library:

```
def add_10(x):
    """
    adds 10 to the input value
```

```
    >>> add_10(5)
    15
    >>> add_10(-2)
    8
    """
    return x + 10

if __name__ == "__main__":
    import doctest
    doctest.testmod()
```

If you run this module from the command line apparently nothing happens. A tweak to the code will illustrate what is going on here. Change the 8 to a 6:

```
def add_10(x):
    """
    adds 10 to the input value
    >>> add_10(5)
    15
    >>> add_10(-2)
    6
    """
    return x + 10

if __name__ == "__main__":
    import doctest
    doctest.testmod()
```

Now when you run it, doctest complains about the 6:

```
**********************************************
File "add10.py", line 7, in __main__.add_10
Failed example:
    add_10(-2)
Expected:
    6
Got:
    8
**********************************************
1 items had failures:
   1 of    2 in __main__.add_10
***Test Failed*** 1 failures.
```

The default behavior of doctest is to remain quiet when everything is fine (or all the tests pass). When something goes wrong, doctest will complain.

Because your test now resides in the docstring, not only does it provide an example of using the API, it becomes testable documentation. As Tim Peters noted in his original post, this can be invaluable when using looking for examples with new code. In fact some projects have used `doctest` to great success, even providing 100% line code coverage for their products with it. (So does that mean their documentation was complete since it effectively tests every line of code?)

integr **doctests**

The same testing done by `unittest` could be done with the following python file, `integrdoctest.py`:

```
"""
This is an explanation of integr
>>> import integr
>>> integr.parse('1,3,4')
[1, 3, 4]

Includes whitespace handling!
>>> integr.parse('1, 3, 4 ')
[1, 3, 4]

Gracefully fails!
>>> integr.parse('abcd')
Traceback (most recent call last):
  ...
BadInput: 'abcd' not valid
"""
if __name__ == "__main__":
    import doctest
    doctest.testmod()
```

If you were developing `integr` with a Python shell open, it would be easy to copy and paste snippets into this doctest along the way.

unittest **or** doctest**?**

At this point you may be asking "which style of testing should I use?" While `unittest` follows a well known paradigm, `doctest` appears to have many benefits. Who wouldn't want documentation, examples and tests?

First of all, using one library does not preclude using the other. However, `doctest` rubs some people the wrong way. It is certainly nice to be able to copy a chunk of interactive code, paste it into a docstring and turn it into a test. But when those chunks are more that a screenful, or those tests end up being longer than the implementation, maybe they are overkill.

As doctest tries to combine documentation, examples and testing, it comes off as a jack-of-all-trades and master-of-none. For example doctest does not include built-in support for setup and teardown, which can make some doctests unnecessarily verbose. Also trying to do extensive testing of corner cases can be distracting when using the docstrings as examples only.

Documentation that contains docstrings can be used by doctest to show illustrate library usage and not necessarily for extensive testing. Using doctest allows easy verification that the documentation is up to date. Later in the life-cycle of the library, as the code evolves and it is time to push a release, it is trivial to verify that the documentation and apis are correct. More extensive testing can be done using unittest (or similar testing frameworks). On the other hand, there are projects that prefer to use doctest everywhere. As with most things in Python, it is easy to try things out.

Organizing doctest files

Do doctests have to reside in code? No. Any text file that contains what looks like a doctest can be used as a test. Some developers like to use unittest for most of their testing, but also like to keep a check that thier documentation is up to date. Mixing both styles makes it easy to accomplish this. To execute the tests found in a file simple run code like so:

```
import doctest
doctest.testfile('/path/to/file')
```

> **Note**
>
> The author of this book uses doctest to test the examples in the source of the book. The third-party docutil library tooling allows easy creation of docu-

> **Note (cont.)**
>
> ments, slides, webpages and handouts that have tested
> Python code.

More fun with doctest

There are a few gotchas with doctest that are good to know
about.

Indentation

Which of the following is correct?

```
>>> print "foo"
foo
>>> print "foo"
    foo
```

The former is the correct one. The latter might look right
but doctest will complain with something like this:

```
Failed example:
    print "foo"
Expected:
        foo
Got:
    foo
```

That error message can be confusing, since it appears to
match what is indicated below Got:. It is important to note
that what is found under Got: is indented!

> **Tip**
>
> If you forget how to line up your output, just try run-
> ning the same code from the interpreter. Since doctest
> is meant to be copied and pasted from interactive ses-
> sions, usually what the interpreter says is correct.

One more thing that might be confusing is that the starting
column of a doctest block does not matter (in fact subsequent

chunks might be indented at a different level). It is assumed that the start of the >>> is the first column for that block. All code for that block should be aligned to that column.

Blanklines

If the following code were in a doctest, the first test would fail. This is because doctest has not yet learned how to read your mind. Is the blank line inserted for clarity or is it actually significant?

```
>>> print ""  # print adds a newline

>>> print "foo"
'foo'
```

To help doctest read your mind, you need to explicitly mark blank lines from that would come from console output with <BLANKLINE>. Try the following instead:

```
>>> print ""  # print adds a newline
<BLANKLINE>
```

Spacing

As you have seen, doctest can be really picky about spacing. One confusing aspect might be when something like the following fails:

```
>>> print range(3)
[0,1,2]
```

When executing the code you would see an error like this:

```
**********************************************
File "/tmp/foo.py", line 4, in __main__.foo
Failed example:
    print range(3)
Expected:
    [0,1,2]
Got:
    [0, 1, 2]
**********************************************
```

Again, doctest expects output to be formatted just like the console, so the spaces folowing the commas are required.

Tip

The doctest module has various directives to tell it to ignore some spacing issues. The #doctest: +NORMALIZE_WHITESPACE directive allows the previous example to work:

```
>>> print range(3)#doctest: +NORMALIZE_WHITESPACE
[1,2,3]
```

Here is one that can leave a developer scratching their head for a while. Say you get the following error in your doctest. What is wrong? (Hint doctest compares characters and this is the "spacing" section)

```
*********************************************
File "/tmp/foo.py", line 6, in __main__.foo
Failed example:
    print range(3)
Expected:
    [0, 1, 2]
Got:
    [0, 1, 2]
*********************************************
```

If you left extra spaces at the end of the expected result, [0, 1, 2]__, (note that there are two spaces at the end of the line, here they are replaced by underscores) instead of [0, 1, 2], you could see this issue.

Dealing with exceptions

Because code can throw exceptions and line numbers have a tendency to change, you do not really want to have to change the line numbers in an exception stack trace every time the code is tweaked. Luckily doctest allows you to replace a stack trace for an exception with . . . :

```
>>> [1, 2, 3].remove(42)
Traceback (most recent call last):
```

```
  ...
ValueError: list.remove(x): x not in list
```

Start Testing

Testing is part of programming. Whether you do it in a formal manner or an ad hoc style, Python has tools suited to aid those efforts.

About the author

Matt Harrison has over 11 years
Python experience across the domains of search, build man-
agement and testing, business intelligence and storage.

He has presented and taught tutorials at conferences such
as SCALE, PyCON and OSCON as well as local user conferences. The structure and content of this book is based off of
first hand experience teaching Python to many individuals.

He blogs at hairysun.com and occasionally tweets useful
Python related information at @__mharrison__.

About the Technical Editor

Shannon -jj Behrens has enjoyed coding in Python for over a
decade. This is the fourth Python book he has edited, but he
has never been brave enough to write his own. In his spare
time, he enjoys chasing after his six children and reading
technical articles his wife sends him on Google+. He blogs
at jjinux.blogspot.com on a wide variety of subjects such as
Python, Ruby, Linux, open source software, the Web, and
lesser-known programming languages.

Index

Made in the USA
Charleston, SC
07 October 2013